T0307931

# THE NARRATIVE
## OF
# LUCY ANN LOBDELL

# THE NARRATIVE

## OF

# LUCY ANN LOBDELL

## A WOMAN'S CASE

### FOR

## EQUALITY

Edited by

## Lisa Macchia Ohliger

WESTHOLME
Yardley

Facing title page: Lucy Ann Lobdell in Native American garb, circa 1850. (*Wayne County [PA] Historical Society*)

©2018 Lisa Macchia Ohliger
Map by Tracy Dungan. ©2018 Westholme Publishing

Westholme Publishing, LLC
904 Edgewood Road
Yardley, Pennsylvania 19067
Visit our Web site at www.westholmepublishing.com

ISBN: 978-1-59416-302-9
Also available as an eBook.

Printed in the United States of America

# CONTENTS

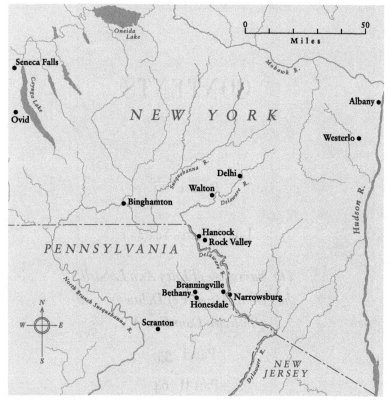

The world of Lucy Ann Lobdell.

# PREFACE

O N OCTOBER 6, 1879, the *New York Times* published an obituary entitled "Death of a Modern
Diana; The Female Hunter of Long Eddy." The
obituary sensationally describes the life of a Lucy Ann Lobdell, living as a vagrant, dressing like a man, and winning
the hearts of ladies. It reads in part:

> In 1851, Lucy Ann Lobdell . . . was married to a
> raftsman named George Slater. She was then 17 years
> old, and was known far and wide for her wonderful
> skill with the rifle . . . in hunting deer and other game
> . . . . After a year of married life, Slater deserted his
> wife and a babe a few weeks old. . . . [She] laid aside
> the habit of her sex, donned male attire, and adopted
> the life of a hunter. . . . For eight years the unfortunate
> wife and mother roamed the woods of that section,
> making her home in the wilderness, where she
> erected crude cabins for her shelter. . . . Her wild life
> was one of thrilling adventure and privation, and it

was not until she was broken down by the exposure and hardships of it that she returned to the haunts of civilization. . . . She wrote a book detailing her adventures in the woods. . . . She recorded in this book that she had killed 168 deer, 77 bears, 1 panther, and numberless wild-cats and foxes.[1]

Beyond the inaccuracies of this depiction lies an even bigger problem—Lucy Ann Lobdell was not dead.

Instead, she suffered a far crueler fate. With her brother claiming that she was uncontrollable due to her refusal to conform to socially acceptable behaviors and gender norms, Lucy was locked away in the Willard Insane Asylum, near Seneca Lake, New York. Despite her violations of local dress codes and vagrancy ordinances, was Lucy really hurting anyone? Newspapers of the time account her life as one of an outsider—a curious, masculine vagrant living in the woods. So, what was it that made her such a target for public harassment and ridicule?

In contemporary literature, Lucy was often portrayed as "strange" or "different" or "before her time." But Lucy Ann Lobdell wasn't before her time. Rather, she exemplified both her time and ours. She was a living example of how antiquated laws, assumptions, and gender boundaries are able to shape, define, and ultimately threaten to destroy the nonconformist.

Lucy was born in 1829 to a sawmill owner and his wife in upstate New York. Andrew Jackson was the newly inaugurated seventh president of the United States, and America was about to embark on a period of vast expansion which would be later attributed to its "Manifest Destiny."

Jackson would advocate this American expansion as "extending the area of freedom."[2] But, as Lucy would discover throughout her life, freedom was not necessarily extended to all.

Lucy's recorded background appears to have begun on January 2, 1853, when a Bridgeport, Connecticut, newspaper published a story written by a "Mr. Talmage," an itinerant peddler. The story of the "Maiden Hunter" cast Lucy into the spotlight, and forged her new identity as a local folk legend. From that point on, Lucy no longer lived a life of anonymity. She was a symbol of sin and deviant behavior, a person for society to make an example of—to punish and to reform.

When Lucy was twenty-six years old, she wrote and self-published a memoir entitled *The Narrative of Lucy Ann Lobdell, the Female Hunter of Delaware and Sullivan Counties, N.Y.* Providing a unique perspective of small-town life along the Upper Delaware River, the *Narrative* recounts her experiences with love, loss, and hardship. She candidly recounts her relationships with family, education, romances, abandonment by an abusive husband, and the choice to meet her own needs in the absence of a provider. In Lucy's words, we see not only her resilience and self-reliance, but also the beginnings of her unconventional life.

On a far more profound scale, Lucy's words are the pragmatic expression of a burgeoning women's rights movement in America. Driven by need and her own will to independently survive, Lucy recognized that her own femininity was an obstacle, preventing her from doing a man's work and earning a man's wages. So, donning a man's clothes, Lucy sought work at a local sawmill so that she was able to provide for her daughter and ailing parents. When Lucy's female identity was revealed, she was cast out.

Lucy's moment in history throws the boundaries of normative gender into question. Some have tried to label Lucy based on her presumed sexuality. She has been called a lesbian, a cross-dresser, or transgender. However, we must ask whether such labels—based largely upon unfounded assumptions about her sexuality—advance our understanding of her life and times. The historical traces of her life instead suggest that her persecution was based not on her sexuality, but rather on her gender.

*The Narrative of Lucy Ann Lobdell: A Woman's Case for Equality* builds on the premise that Lucy's battle was not limited to her personally, but was one that women still fight today. Women throughout history have brought about change in what were considered normative gender roles and what was deemed socially acceptable. This book focuses on the societal practices that reflected gender inequality. I shift attention away from Lucy's modern label of transgender and instead take a historical approach that focuses on laws, religious practices, the foundations of the women's rights movement, and how these important factors influenced Lucy and many other women of her time.

Through the use of historical society archives, newspaper clippings, court documents, legal and medical records, academic research, and Lucy's own *Narrative*—presented here in its entirety—we can piece together much of Lucy's tumultuous life and see why this unassuming woman has been a fascinating subject for so many.

# LUCY'S EARLY YEARS

The *Narrative of Lucy Ann Lobdell, the Female Hunter of Delaware and Sullivan Counties, N.Y.* was written in 1855 by Lucy Lobdell, deserted wife and mother of one. We can only speculate why she felt the need to pen her own autobiography at the young age of twenty-six. Women of this time, having limited rights, were left with very few outlets to share their stories. Obviously, Lucy felt she had a story worth telling. She would live to the age of eighty-three, leaving us to wonder about those missing fifty years between 1855 and 1912. We can only piece together her life with scraps of newspaper clippings and oral histories, sewn together like the crazy quilts of her era.

Lucy's *Narrative* is composed of two parts. The first is a glimpse into her everyday life, her struggles with family, and the hardships they faced. The second part focuses on the "female hunter" legend and how this persona affected her life. The second part includes a promise from Lucy to write a continuation of her life story, but this never comes to fruition. Lucy self-published her *Narrative* through an unknown printer in upstate New York. The price for a copy of her forty-seven-page booklet was fifty cents, which for many amounted to half a week's wages.

It is not known how many copies of Lucy's *Narrative* were printed or where they were sold. There are only two known copies in public record: one in the Yale University Library in New Haven, Connecticut, and the other in the archives of the Wayne County Historical Society in Honesdale, Pennsylvania.

## The *Narrative*, Part I

On December 2, 1829, Sarah (Sally) and James Lobdell welcomed the birth of their daughter Lucy Ann. Lucy was an answered prayer for Sarah and James, who had lost their first-born daughter to illness as a toddler. Infant mortality rates were high due to outbreaks of typhoid fever, smallpox, tuberculosis, and other infections. It was expected that about 25 percent of children born at this time in the United States would not see their fifth birthday.[1] The Lobdell's first daughter was no exception: "This little innocent was born but to bloom for a few short months upon earth, before her Heavenly Father called her to himself. . . . She had just begun to lisp the endearing words—Father! Mother!—just budded in infantile beauty and sportiveness, when the stern mandate was issued; and disease attacked the delicate frame. . . . She was two years, one month, and ten days old when she died."

Although she never knew her older sister, Lucy recognized the impact of her death upon her own childhood:

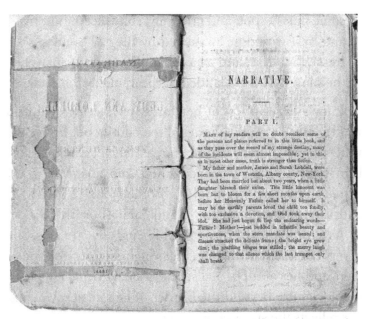

The opening spread of the *Narrative of Lucy Ann Lobdell, Female Hunter of Delaware and Sullivan Counties, N.Y.*, 1855. (*Wayne County [PA] Historical Society*)

As I was the only living child, it is not strange that I became their pet—almost a spoiled child. . . . And now for an incident, here and there, as that faithful friend may bring before me those happy days of youth. When care was a stranger, I was oftentimes strolling the little wood that was but a short distance from my home, and oft did I get lost chasing and searching for the little Robin red-breast as she warbled her lays at morn and eve; and, now and then, stopping to cull the wild flowers that thronged my pleasant pathway, till, tired and weary, I sank upon some mossy spot, and cried myself to sleep. But, by and by, I would be awakened by the call of my distressed mother; and away I would hurry to answer the summons, and gladden the heart of that fond one.

Lucy's description of her forest wanderings paints a vivid picture of her rather carefree childhood, under the watchful eye of her protective parents. Her reminiscence brings her feelings of peacefulness and nostalgia. Lucy would ultimately be joined by brother John (born 1832) and sisters Mary (born 1836) and Sarah (born 1838).

As a teen, Lucy shows signs of being adventurous. She is very confident in many subjects including school, young men, and her outdoor skills. She is a daydreamer, imagining adventure beyond the border of her small town, and she reflects the spirit of her times.

Time passes, and I hurry to my fourteenth year, and again find an observation. I was then at school, and possessed a temperament which made me foremost in mischief as well as in study. My delight in each was about equal. I was ever and anon trying to get my lesson, and, at the same time, thinking and acting mischief together. . . . It happened one night I was at a spelling-class that my train of thought was to take a different direction, for after school was dismissed, a Mr. William Smith asked to see me safe home. I at once took his offered arm, and away we tripped homeward, chatting and laughing at some foolish remark we might mistake for wit and sentiment. We at length were getting to be the objects of remark, as day after day passed in its turn; and we arranged business of almost every day so as to have an interview, which we would ofttimes while away in telling and laughing over the news of the day.

W hen Lucy was a girl, the Lobdells and much of their extended family lived around Westerlo, New York, one of four small rural towns in the Helderberg region about eleven miles southwest of Albany. The Helderberg Escarpment, upon which these towns are situated, rises to 2,000 feet above the Hudson Valley. Westerlo, also known as Thayer's Corners, contained little more than a general store and blacksmith shop. The Helderberg region saw the establishment of general stores and grist and sawmills beginning in the late eighteenth century. Lucy's grandfather, Isaac Lobdell, built one of the first grist mills in the area on Basic Creek in 1795.[2] His mill was very successful and helped spark the construction of other local mills. Lucy's family were ordinary farmers like many in the area, but farming was extremely difficult there due to the rocky soil. Many had no choice but to abandon their fields and seek work in the mills.

Difficulties with rocks were not the only sources of hardship for this agricultural community. The shift toward an industrial economy during the nineteenth century made farming throughout the United States a struggle. In an effort to remain relevant and profitable, family farmers had to utilize new technology, employ more laborers, and incur more debt in order to increase their production. The result, nationally, was tremendous yields which flooded mar-

One-room school house in Westerlo, New York. Photograph Postcard. Lucy learned how to read and write at this school.

kets. This overproduction caused prices to fall sharply, precipitating the steady decline of not only an industry, but also a way of life.

The shift from agrarian to industrial life marked a sea change in the American economy. Mass production in factories rendered the rural artisan obsolete, further adding to the economic stress upon communities like those in the Helderberg region. From 1830 to 1910, Westerlo's population steadily decreased from over 3,300 to about 1,300 residents. Simultaneously, the population of New York City exploded from 242,278 to 4,766,833. Even the population of nearby Albany increased from 24,209 to 101,253 during the eighty-year measure of Lucy's lifetime.[3]

Federal census data further reveals that James, Sarah, and their four children remained on their family farm in Westerlo until the 1850s. James's real estate holdings during that time were valued at about $2,000 (the equivalent of approximately $60,000 in 2018).[4] James also sought work in the local mills, and he sold lumber to the asheries. Asheries, gristmills, sawmills, carding mills, and cloth dressing mills supported the local economy and families like the Lobdells.

Sarah Lobdell, like many women of the time, maintained the homestead. If opportunity allowed, she earned additional money cleaning houses. Employment for women was usually confined to extensions of their domestic responsibilities. Thus domestic services, teaching, nursing, and the clothing trade were common jobs for women outside the home. Some middle-class women were hired as governesses for upper-class families, but these positions were limited. Women were typically paid poorly, as their employment was generally considered low status and involving fewer skills than men's work. However, among the poor, men and women were forced to do whatever was necessary to survive.

Small rural towns such as Westerlo offered little opportunity for experience or training in professional trades. Most trades were learned through family members or apprenticeships. Post-elementary education was relatively rare in these towns, where surviving and maintaining the family farm or business took precedence. James learned to farm from his father and uncles before working in the mills. He would eventually own a sawmill and teach that trade to Lucy's brother John.

While higher learning could not always be of priority to rural farmers, many families during this time understood that even rural industry had to compete with business in larger urban areas. As the ability to write and read contracts and interact with buyers and manufacturers was essential, education and literacy steadily increased in importance.

The nineteenth-century school experience varied considerably. Children in small rural communities were taught in one-room schoolhouses, where they learned reading, writing, arithmetic, and moral principles. Some larger towns had academies, and cities typically had larger schools enrolling several hundred students. Attendance was voluntary, but a fairly large percentage of children attended school. It is estimated that, during the 1830s, 90 percent of all non-urban youth in New York State attended school at least part-time.[5] A child's school years might be intermittent, especially for older students who often attended in winter and worked on farms during the remainder of the year.

When Lucy was fourteen, she was regulary attending a local district school in Westerlo. Lucy recollects fond memories of primary school, and boasts of her academic skills: "I would frequently contrive, during the hours of study, to read from another book, which I would conceal from the teacher's eye, and still have my lesson more perfect than half the scholars who were more studious, but less vivacious."

Many children in Lucy's time concluded their education at the fifth grade. In addition to the obligations of the farm, secondary schooling often came with a tuition bill that most families could not afford. Lucy's parents supported her desire to continue her education but were unable to afford tuition. Self-reliant and determined, Lucy raised her own tuition and entered the Coxsackie School in Greene County, New York. As she recounts: "I was in my tenth or twelfth year when I had the charge of some hundred chickens, turkeys, and geese, that I used to raise and sell, and then I had half the money I made in that business and in tending the dairy; and so when I went to Coxsackie, I had money I had made raising calves and poultry to pay for my schooling, and all the expenses I incurred in going to school."

While she was right to be proud of her accomplishment in securing her own education, Lucy's opportunity to do so was no doubt aided by New York's progressive effort to legislatively promote, subsidize, and centralize education. The Common School Act of 1812 shaped the future of public education in New York by establishing that (1) common schools were a state function under state control; (2) funding of public schools was a joint state-local responsibility; (3) the school district—not the county or the town— was the primary administrative unit for public education.[6]

Promoting education in poor rural areas remained a focus of New York's educational system well into the twentieth century, and was further achieved by raising teaching standards and extending the school year. The 1840s saw vast improvement in school administration, teacher training, school curriculum, and the overall improvement of conditions—especially in the one-room school. Major steps were taken in the 1850s to expand the state's financial assistance to the poorer rural school districts. Along with this money came an effort to eliminate tuition fees that made attending school more difficult or impossible for poorer students. Most cities eliminated tuition fees in the 1840s and 1850s, and tuition was ended statewide in 1867 thanks to many parents and teachers lobbying for tuition-free common schools.

Despite these great strides toward equal access to education by eliminating socioeconomic barriers, opportunities were not the same for the genders. While young women had some access to secondary education, they were largely excluded from universities. The first American university to admit a female student was Oberlin College in 1837.

The effort to standardize education in New York was no small feat. With a rapidly growing population in the northern and western regions of the state, many students were required to travel and find lodging with extended family or in boarding houses in order to attend these schools. We can assume from the twenty-mile distance between Westerlo and the Coxsackie School that Lucy was not immune to these challenges. Travel was by horse-drawn carriage, and even the relatively short distance from Westerlo to Coxsackie took several hours. In the *Narrative* she mentions staying with an aunt while at school.

Although Lucy seems to have been well focused on her education, she was also preoccupied with a boy who briefly courted her back home. On their first encounter, George Washington Slater seemed to be a quiet, agreeable young man. Lucy, apparently feeling sorry for his lack of family and friends, decided to befriend George, and they kept each other's company for nearly six months. During this time, George seems to have fallen in love with Lucy, although Lucy protested his advances and noted her father's disapproval. When George fell ill at one point, Lucy dressed in her brother's clothes and rode off on her father's horse to check on his well-being. This is the first instance that Lucy mentions dressing in men's clothing, simply to avoid detection as a woman riding alone at night. It was not the last time that she would resort to dressing as a man to achieve a practical goal.

During the nineteenth century, women commonly married in their teens. In addition to being socially expected, this eased the financial burden on families raising young women. But young women were not to focus too obviously on finding a husband. Being "forward" in the company of men suggested a worrisome sexual appetite, and women were assumed to marry because it allowed them to become mothers rather than to pursue sexual or emotional satisfaction.

Lucy was well aware that being seen regularly with a man with no proposal of marriage could lead to trouble. At this time it was common practice to remind prepubescent girls of their special vulnerability to sexual misconduct. A young woman frequently sighted with a man who was not her husband ran the risk of being accused of having sexual relations out of wedlock. The young woman, and not her male companion, would be held responsible for both the sin and the possible consequences. Young women had the burden of repressing not only their own sexual urges, but also those of their partners. Lucy seemed conflicted about her feelings for George, but she also knew what was expected of her: "I felt I knew not how; but, in other words, that I was forming an acquaintance with Mr. Slater that I might repent if not carefully looked after."

At this point Lucy left for the Coxsackie School, where she stayed for one to two years. Although she was there to continue her education, she could not seem to get George off of her mind: "Well, time passed slowly away, and I had not heard one syllable from my George since I left home."

It is obvious that she was somewhat lovestruck and hoping that George continued to court her. She returned home on a small break from school, only to find that George was not there waiting. She quite dramatically states: "The charm was gone while the charmer was absent. Memory of the old times made the present distasteful." She went back to school with a heavy heart, believing that George had found a new love interest.

In what seems to be an attempt to run from her heartache, Lucy (now eighteen years old), wrote to her father from Coxsackie asking him to move from Westerlo to an area on the Delaware River near Hancock, New York. Regarding Westerlo, she noted that: "Memory of the old times made the present distasteful. I could not bear to stay there. . . . Father wrote and said if I wanted to live at Coxsackie he would sell out and come and buy there, if I wanted him to."

Lucy told her father about a dream she had of the Delaware River, and of the vast virginal woodlands "selling very cheap." The Upper Delaware River was home to a vibrant logging industry, so James, like many other farmers, sold his farmland and heeded the call of the forest.

The Lobdells settled in Rock Valley, a few miles southeast of Hancock, New York. Hancock is a small river
town at the confluence of the east and west branches of the
Delaware River, about forty miles east of Binghamton and
one hundred miles southwest of Westerlo, and one of the
earliest settlements in Delaware County, New York. James
Lobdell saw promise in the Delaware and adjacent Sullivan
County woods and found a property that suited his plans.
He would prove to be a driving force in the development
of Rock Valley, and was reputedly responsible for building
the town's first meetinghouse (which also served as a
church and the area's first school).

As an industry, logging gained momentum after the Revolutionary War. Before the lumbering industry came, much
of Delaware and Sullivan Counties were untouched and
the land was wild. There were few roads and much of the
area was still inhabited by Native Americans. Some towns
along the river were only accessible by boat. The railroad
was a new form of transportation at this time, and only the
most industrialized small towns had stations on New York's
Erie Railroad that crossed the state. Timber was harvested
in the upriver forests and sent for use in the growing cities.
Amidst the transportation revolution (roads, canals, railroad), port towns like Hancock had direct access to New
York City and Philadelphia. It is estimated that over 50 mil-
lion board feet of pine and hemlock were shipped annually
down the Delaware. The timber industry was also instrumental in the development of the tanning industry in the
area. Along the river, remnants of the sawmills and tanneries
that built the region still can be found.

James was fortunate to have had the ability to purchase property from the proceeds of the sale of his farm in Westerlo. At this time, most workers lived on small parcels in town, large enough only for a kitchen garden and animal stall. Many also rented small shacks from their employers. From what little we know about James's Rock Valley property, it appears to have contained a log cabin constructed in 1852.[7] The plot he purchased, though, was large enough to support livestock and had ample trees for fuel and logging. Days were filled with hard labor, farming, and caring for the homestead. James built his own sawmill to process cherry, pine, and hemlock, which he then shipped to Philadelphia on Hemlock rafts. This proved to be a lucrative business for the Lobdell family, and one that James's son John would continue.

After living in Rock Valley for a year, Lucy was reunited with George Slater. He asked for her hand in marriage, and Lucy accepted. George and Lucy tried to begin a life together in their new settlement on the Delaware, but Lucy didn't know many people in the area other than her close family. In her effort to build a support system within the community, Lucy turned to the church. Lucy appears deeply devout and often speaks of her belief in God in her *Narrative*. At one point, Lucy and George attended the sermon of a local Methodist preacher. When the preacher asked if "one sinner wished or would rise to have the brethren pray for him," George rose. And as Lucy recounts, "I also rose on seeing his wish to become a Christian."

Religion was an important part of an early settler's social life. The town meetinghouse often doubled as a gathering

A one-room school house, top, and church and meetinghouse, bottom, in Rock Valley, New York. Both were built on James Lobdell's land. The church and meetinghouse are now private residences. (*Ohliger*)

place and the local church. Dances, quilting circles, and other social events were held there. Ultimately, George and Lucy became members of the Methodist church in Hancock, but she tells us that her "sentiments varied from theirs with regard to their belief very much." While she does not further elaborate on these differences, we know that Lucy would have been influenced by the Quaker and Shaker ideas so prevalent in upstate New York at the time.

The first Shaker settlement was purchased in 1776 in Albany. The Shaker roots are based in that of The Society of Friends, or Quaker ideology. Many Quaker and Shaker beliefs were seen as radical when compared to the strict religious conventions of the Puritans and the Church of England. Quaker founder George Fox believed everyone shared a part of God's "inner light," and a personal experience with God's salvation. Quakers had no formal religious practices or ceremonies. There was no clergy or pulpit. They gathered in a simple meetinghouse with rows of benches. No one spoke unless inspired by God. Both men and women were encouraged to speak when "moved" on any subject.

Most important to our understanding of Lucy is the central Quaker belief in the equality of all people. Men and women are perceived as equal in all respects, and this belief is seen in not only their practices, but their political and social influence as well. Shaker beliefs were similar to those of the Quakers, though decidedly stricter. Shakers' religious ideals required a life of celibacy, communal living, equality of the sexes, and pacifism. Both Quakers and Shakers devoted their lives to work and worship. They were committed to creating a society that was equal for all, regardless of gender or race. They believed God was both male and female in character, so men and women shared power in the community.[8]

Quaker and Shaker ideology undoubtedly influenced the social movements of the nineteenth century, including the temperance, Native American rights, women's rights, and abolitionist movements. Prominent female Quakers included Lucretia Mott, Jane Hunt, Martha Wright, and Mary Ann M'Clintock, founders of the first Women's Rights Convention in Seneca Falls, New York, in 1848. Given Lucy's location and education, her exposure to these beliefs would have been unavoidable.

### The *Narrative*, Part II

In Part II of her *Narrative*, Lucy recalls the "hunting stories" from her youth: "In consequence in keeping poultry, I learned to shoot hawk, weasel, the mink, and even down to the rat."

She recounted her many accidental adventures in the Delaware and Sullivan County woods while hunting deer. She had so many hunting stories to share—wild chases, getting lost in the woods—that she explains: "I shall be obliged to pass over some hundred little hunting adventures, and give them a place in my next book."

Unfortunately, her pleasant pastime was eventually soured by an account published in the *Bridgeport Standard* on February 2, 1853. In it, a traveling peddler named Talmage described a female dressed in men's clothing with remarkable marksmanship. Talmage was invited to the

Lobdell home, where he witnessed what he calls "the maiden-hunter" caring for her ailing parents and performing all the farm's chores, playing the violin most excellently, and returning to the woods to hunt again. This caricature was circulated in a few of the regional newspapers, and Lucy quickly became a folk legend in an era when word of mouth easily lent itself to hyperbole. Folktales tend to capture and reflect society's shared fears and fantasies, and offer us insight into the attitudes of the period. Although Lucy did certainly hunt, accounts involving her slaying panthers and hundreds of deer are surely embellished.

In 1890, London's *Illustrated Police News* published the following, entitled "A Strange Story":

> In a book entitled "The Life and Adventures of Lucy Ann Lobdell, the Female Hunter of Long Eddy," written by herself after relinquishing her wild life, many thrilling incidents are related that occurred in her experience in the woods.
>
> Among these are the details of a hand-to-hand contest with a panther, which attacked her after she had wounded it near Mongaup Pond, in Sullivan county. She killed the animal, but received such injuries that she was unable to get away from her cabin, which chanced to be near, for several days.
>
> One time she shot a huge panther after a long and fatiguing tramp. The panther reared on its haunches and started for her with distended jaws. Feeling that she was too much worn with her tramp to brave the fury of the panther at close quarters, she ran to a small tree near by, intending to climb beyond reach of the

wounded animal. She clasped her arms about the tree and fainted away. When she recovered consciousness she was still clasping the tree. Recalling the circumstances that preceded her running to the tree, she looked about her. About ten feet away the panther lay stretched on the ground dead. Her ball had entered its vitals and done its work before the animal reached her.[9]

No autobiographical record exists of this account of Lucy's slaying of a panther, let alone the vivid description of the surrounding events and circumstances. Her only known writing is her *Narrative*, which is not the title cited in the article.

Such embellishments are not unique to Lucy's story, as panther slaying is a theme of the time used to emphasize the prowess of a hunter. In an oral history of Dyberry Township of Wayne County, Pennsylvania, a Mrs. Simons recalls a tale of her grandfather being stalked by a panther. She recalls a local hunter, Mr. Teeple, who killed the panther and a long list of other animals. But it was Mr. Teeple's slaying of the panther that underscored his reputation as a great hunter.[10]

The *Illustrated Police News* article continued, in further apparent exaggeration, with an account of Lucy's incarcerations and court proceedings in Honesdale, Pennsylvania:

> Lucy Ann, or "Joe" as she is called, has several times been in gaol [jail] in Honesdale lately for vagrancy, and her companion hovers about the prison until her "husband" is released. The last time "Joe"

was in gaol "his" companion drew up a petition to
the Court, covering several pages of foolscap, and
written with a split stick with the juice of pokeberries,
praying for "his" release. The document is preserved
in the Court records and is a marvel of neat penman-
ship, choice diction, and ingenious argument. The
woman who wrote it, and who now lives the life of an
outcast in companionship with a crazy, filthy, and dis-
eased fellow-being, is a graduate of the Massachusetts
Female College. Their abode near this place is a miserable hovel in the woods.[11]

A search of Wayne County court dockets failed to reveal
even a hint of these proceedings or events. It appears that
Lucy was never the subject of any court case in Wayne
County, and it is unclear whether she was ever held at the
county jail for any extended period of time. Unfortunately,
sheriff's logs which may help to confirm whether she was
held there for any period no longer exist.

The written plea of Lucy's female "companion" to the
court is lifted from an article entitled "A Mountain Romance," published in the *New York Times* over a decade
before, on April 8, 1877, where she is identified as "Mrs.
Wilson":

There is on record now in the courts of Wayne
County a document that was drawn by Mrs. Wilson,
the companion of Lucy Ann, it being a petition for
the release of her "husband, Joseph I. Lobdell" from
jail, on account of "his" failing health. The pen used
by the writer was a stick whittled to a point and split;

the ink was pokeberry juice. The writing is faultless, and the language used a model of clear, correct, and argumentative English—a really superior piece of composition, showing that the writer, now a voluntary outcast and the associate of an insane, foul, and unsexed woman, is highly educated, and capable of adorning the best circles.[12]

Other than the mere proclamation that the document exists, there is nothing in the *New York Times* article to indicate that its writer had seen the document or otherwise confirmed its existence. An obituary of Lucy was published in the *Wayne Independent* on October 16, 1879, two years after the *New York Times* article. The obituary was erroneous, since Lucy would not die until May 28, 1912. In it, a similar, though even less detailed account of Marie Wilson's "petition" is given: "The Wilson woman wrote a petition to the court for the release of her 'husband' using a piece of split wood for a pen and poke berry juice for ink."[13]

So, each account of the "petition" makes only vague reference to its content and instead fixates on the quaint manner in which it was supposedly written. Even the author of the obituary in the local *Wayne Independent*, who would have had ready access to the court's docket, fails to cite any specific content which would tend to verify that the document was viewed and its existence confirmed.

Thus, the accuracy of this dramatic account, of Lucy's "wife" waiting for her dutifully outside of the county jail and penning pokeberry juice letters to plead for her release, is doubtful. However, this questionable story does arguably serve a purpose within the context of Lucy's emerging legend—feminizing Marie Wilson and painting her as the dutiful wife of a scoundrel "husband" whose bizarre behavior often lands "him" in jail. Regardless of the truth or falsity of any specific claim, these articles are typical of the sensational accounts of Lucy's life. Such articles were printed in newspapers throughout the United States and beyond. This newfound fame was unwelcome, as Lucy had become so accustomed to living as she wished in the comfort and privacy of the wilderness. Now, her hunting grounds "were infested with hunters" as people became curious about the life of this so-called "Maiden-Hunter."

The tale of Lucy is eventually picked up by the *Philadelphia Press*, which claimed to publish the "first accurate account of the life of this remarkable woman." The article, entitled "Crack Shot. The Story of the Female Hunter of Long Eddy," paints a likeness of Lucy as an "attractive woman with masculine traits." This is similar to the itinerant peddler Talmage's earlier account in the *Bridgeport Standard*, in which he observed: "I was overtaken by what I, at first, supposed was a young man, with a rifle on his shoulder. . . . Although I can not give a very clear idea of her appearance, I will try to describe her dress. The only article of female apparel visible was a close-fitting hood upon her head, such as is often worn by deer hunters; next, an India-rubber over-coat. Her nether limbs were encased in a pair of snug-fitting corduroy pants, and a pair of Indian moccasins were upon her feet."[14]

These accounts of Lucy's appearance seem to be belied by a contemporary photograph believed to be of her (see page ii). While this photograph may very well depict a rural woman not accustomed to city living, there is nothing particularly "masculine" about her appearance. One must therefore question whether the accounts of Talmage and the *Philadelphia Press* are accurate portrayals, or simply matters of gender stereotyping. As the sensationalism of Lucy's story lies in her undertaking the typically male activity of hunting, we must ask whether her appearance is being transformed in legend to correlate with her unconventional gender role.

Further support for the notion that her masculinity may have been exaggerated is found in the "Female Hunter" moniker and her similarities to Artemis. The Greek goddess of the hunt and moon roamed the wilderness armed with a bow and quiver. Artemis, and her Roman equivalent Diana, represent adventure, athletics, independence, and solitude. Another premature obituary of Lucy appeared in the *New York Times* on October 7, 1879:

DEATH OF A MODERN DIANA: THE FEMALE HUNTER OF LONG EDDY

The Strange Life-History of Lucy Slater—Her Career as a Huntress, a Pauper, a Minister, and a Vagrant—Dressed in Man's Clothing She Wins a Girl's Love.

DELHI, N.Y., Oct 6.—News of the death of Lucy Ann Lobdell Slater, known throughout the Delaware Valley as the "Female Hunter of Long Eddy," has been received here, and it recalls a most singular life-history. . . . In 1851, Lucy Ann Lobdell . . . was married to a raftsman named George Slater. She was then 17 years old, and was known far and wide for her wonderful skill with the rifle . . . in hunting deer and other game. . . . After a year of married life, Slater deserted his wife and a babe a few weeks old . . . [she] laid aside the habit of her sex, donned male attire, and adopted the life of a hunter. . . . For eight years the unfortunate wife and mother roamed the woods of that section, making her home in the wilderness, where she erected crude cabins for her shelter. . . . Her wild life was one of thrilling adventure and privation, and it was not until she was broken down by the exposure and hardships of it that she returned to the haunts of civilization. . . . She wrote a book detailing her adventures in the woods. . . . She recorded in this book that she had killed 168 deer, 77 bears, 1 panther, and numberless wild-cats and foxes.[15]

Of course, Lucy gives no such account in her *Narrative*. But the purpose of this account, to draw the parallels between Lucy and Artemis and to lend them to her sensational legend, is well served by this exaggerated account. This false obituary then goes on to describe her declining physical and mental health, and her relationship with Marie Louise Perry Wilson as follows:

A strong affection sprang up between the two women, notwithstanding the difference in their habits, character, and intellect. They refused to be separated, and in the Spring of 1869 they left the Poor-house together, and for two years they were not heard from in Delhi. In the Summer of the above year a couple calling themselves the Rev. Joseph Israel

Lobdell and wife appeared in the mountain villages of Monroe County, Penn. For two years they roamed about that section, living in caves and cabins in the woods, subsisting on game, berries, and on the charity of the lumbering foresters scattered about in this region. They generally appeared at the settlements leading a bear which they had tamed.

Lucy's accompaniment by a tamed bear is unsupported by any known eyewitness account. But it is readily understood when we look at the long association between Artemis and the bear. Here is a description from the *Suda*, a tenth-century Byzantine encyclopedia:

Arktos e Brauroniois (I was a bear at the Brauronia): Women playing the bear used to celebrate a festival for Artemis dressed in saffron robes; not older than 10 years nor less than 5; appeasing the goddess. The reason was that a wild she-bear used to come to the deme of Phlauidoi and spend time there; and she became tamed and was brought up with the humans. Some virgin was playing with her and, when the girl began acting recklessly, the she-bear was provoked and scratched the virgin; her brothers were angered by this and speared the she-bear, and because of this a pestilential sickness fell upon the Athenians. When the Athenians consulted the oracle [the god] said that there would be a release from the evils if, as blood price for the she-bear that died, they compelled their virgins to play the bear. And the Athenians decreed that no virgin might be given in marriage to a man if she hadn't previously played the bear for the goddess.[16]

Thus, the obituary writer who referred to Lucy as a "modern Diana" would have appreciated the significance of pairing her with a tamed bear when emerging from the wilderness with her wife, alarming the townspeople.

Jungian psychologists would later discuss archetypes as "collective universal patterns or motifs which come from the collective unconscious and are the basic content of religions, mythologies, legends, and fairytales."[17] An archetype can be said to express the presence of a divine force within the human soul that manifests itself in all the typical human patterns of thought, emotions, imagery, and behavior.

The Artemis archetype is said to emerge in women as an innate sense of social justice, a desire for equality with men, and a sisterhood with women. Due to their "masculine" energy and ability, neither Lucy nor Artemis needed a male counterpart—an inconceivable concept for most of nineteenth-century America. (The recognition of two women cohabitating was a feature of Henry James's 1886 novel, *The Bostonians*.) It is therefore clear that references to Lucy as the "Female Hunter," "Maiden Hunter," and "modern Diana" were no accident. Authors of these accounts observed these parallels to Artemis, even if their intent may have been to exploit and sensationalize these similarities.

Further adding to Lucy's notoriety was the depiction of George Slater as having deserted his wife. In an effort to cull these rumors and justify his departure, George claimed that Lucy took part in "sprees" and was frequently in the company of other men. Unable to provide financially for her family, Lucy decided to leave her parents and young daughter—slipping away early one morning under cover of darkness. This was a painful parting for Lucy, but something that she saw as essential for their survival: "I could not even kiss my little Helen, nor tell her how her mother was going to seek employment to get a little spot to live, and earn something for her as she grew up. So, I stole away with a heavy heart, for I knew that I was going among strangers, who did not know my circumstances, or see my heart, so broken, and know its struggles."

Lucy sought work outside of the area where she was so well known, so that she could better conceal her identity while laboring in male attire. Her hope was to gain employment to help support her family. Many commentators, including scholars, writers, and doctors, have attempted to reconcile Lucy's decision to dress as a man as evidence that she was transgender or homosexual. However, Lucy was explicit that her purpose was gainful employment. While it is certainly possible that Lucy may have been transgender or homosexual (or perhaps both), there is simply no evidence of this in her *Narrative*.

Instead, what we clearly can see reflected in Lucy's experience is the rigid gender roles of nineteenth-century America. The view that women and men possessed distinct characteristics was universally held, and derived from religious ideology, science, and medicine of the time. Men were perceived as naturally aggressive, while women were passive. Thus, men were thought to be more prone to com-

mit crimes (especially violent ones), while women's crimes
were in the realm of aberrant behavior.

On the subject of criminality, many states had laws
against a person appearing in public in attire not belonging
to his or her sex. Laws against cross-dressing became a tool
for local police to enforce societal gender norms and to
suppress social change. In response to this societal oppres-
sion, Lucy concludes her *Narrative* with a rallying cry for
women's right to equality: "Help, one and all, to aid
woman, the weaker vessel. If she is willing to toil, give her
wages equal with that of a man. And as in sorrow she bears
her own curse, (nay, indeed, she helps to bear a man's burden also,) secure to her her rights, or permit her to wear
the pants, and breathe the pure air of heaven, and you stay
and be convinced at home with the children how pleasant
a task it is to act the part that woman must act."

Of course, the women's rights movement gained momentum in the late nineteenth century, as women began to
rebel against their perceived inferiority based on traditional
gender roles. Women were coming to realize that, in order
to be effective social reformers, they first needed to acquire
legal rights. They could no longer be viewed as dependents
of men, without the power to bring a suit, make contracts,
own property, or vote. Significant gains were made in these
areas while Lucy was a young woman. In 1848, women in
New York saw a major victory with the passing of the Married Women's Property Act. The act allowed a married
woman, without permission from her husband, to own
property: "The real and personal property, of any female
now married shall not be subject to the disposal of her hus-

The Seneca Falls Trio: Lucretia Mott, Susan B. Anthony, Elizabeth Cady Stanton. (*New York Public Library*)

band; but shall be her sole and separate property as if she were a single female."[18]

Women could now buy, sell, bequeath, and receive rent for property—all foundational to potential financial independence. In that same year, the Seneca Falls Convention was held to discuss the "social, civil, and religious condition and rights of woman" and was the first of its kind. Elizabeth Cady Stanton drafted the "Declaration of Sentiments, Grievances, and Resolutions," modeled after the Declaration of Independence, listing all the forms of discrimination and injustices inflicted upon women.

The women's rights movement demanded change in laws regarding the right to elective franchise, child custody, divorce, education, property rights, and equal pay. During the first day the convention was exclusively for women, while on the second day, some forty men were invited to attend, including the abolitionist Frederick Douglass. Just days after the convention, the participants would be brutally ridiculed in the press. National newspapers proclaimed the "Declaration of Sentiments" to be shameless, and criticized the audacity of women to demand the right to vote. This smear campaign ultimately backfired, helping to expand the movement by relaying the news of these grievances to women across the country. The Seneca Falls Convention was followed two weeks later by an even larger meeting in Rochester. After Rochester, the movement spread rapidly and conventions would be held annually.

One of the many observers at the convention in Seneca Falls was Amelia Bloomer, a proponent of the temperance movement. Although Bloomer was too conservative in her beliefs to sign the Declaration of Sentiments, her presence on the second day would foster a bond between herself, Stanton, and Susan B. Anthony for many years. Ultimately this friendship would encourage Bloomer to publish the women's newspaper the *Lily: A Monthly Journal, Devoted to Temperance and Literature*.

Amelia Bloomer was married to Dexter Bloomer, a Quaker reformist, law student, and co-owner of the *Seneca County Courier*. Dexter gave Amelia an opportunity to write for the *Courier*, and would ultimately help her start up the *Lily*. The *Lily* was originally conceived by Amelia as a publication for the women's temperance movement, but gradually the newspaper expanded to include women's rights and the writings of Elizabeth Cady Stanton.

Amelia herself began to write on women's rights issues, including dress reform. She advocated for women to wear what was then called the "Bloomer costume," which was influenced by the Turkish pants worn by Elizabeth Cady Stanton's cousin, Elizabeth Smith Miller. After working in her garden and becoming "thoroughly disgusted with the long skirt," Miller started wearing the trousers in 1851.[19] "Bloomers" allowed women to perform daily activities with ease. Amelia would pen an article in the *Lily* on women's trousers, along with pictures of herself wearing this new fashion-forward garb.

Amelia Bloomer wearing a short dress with pants underneath. (*National Park Service*)

The *Lily* was distributed throughout the East, and would have been accessible to Lucy Lobdell. Within a year, its circulation increased from about 300 to over 800, and would quickly gain thousands of subscribers. Women such as Lucy, whose social protest was previously limited to their thoughts and private actions, were now finding new, more public outlets, including the clothes they wore. One 1871 newspaper account about Lucy (highlighting her seemingly uncontrolled behavior) was entitled "The Lady in Pantaloons."[20]

But Lucy's struggle was a much more private one than a reflection of the monumental changes of her time. At the close of her *Narrative*, Lucy tells a story filled with sorrow about her marriage, home, and family devastated by alcoholism.

The mother marks that staggering form as he wends his way to the bed whereon he goes to sleep and forgets the care he now throws away in the whirl of drunkenness. Mother clings tighter to that babe, and cries to that Being of Wisdom to enable her to bear the ills that thus betide her. Well, we will follow yet a little farther. We behold that the father has squandered all his living in drunkenness. He has become a drunkard; his home is now a hovel of wretchedness and misery. The mother is obliged to toil, day by day, for her little ones, and she scarcely get a morsel of food for herself, as she will toil and feed on the crumbs. And, now, we see again that mother has fallen. Her babes are left to the charity of the world.

Amid her guilt and sadness, she suggests the possibility of a second book. But because of the personal struggles that followed, that sequel was never written.

# NARRATIVE

# LUCY ANN LOBDELL,

THE

# FEMALE HUNTER

OF

## DELAWARE AND SULLIVAN COUNTIES, N. Y.

NEW-YORK:
PUBLISHED FOR THE AUTHORESS.
1855.

*Narrative of Lucy Ann Lobdell, Female Hunter of Delaware and Sullivan Counties, N.Y., 1855. Original Cover. (Wayne County [PA] Historical Society)*

# Narrative.

---

## Part I.

Many of my readers will no doubt recollect some of the persons and places referred to in this little book, and as they pass over the record of my strange destiny, many of the incidents will seem almost impossible; yet in this, as in most other cases, truth is stranger than fiction.

My Father and Mother, James and Sarah Lobdell, were born in the town of Westerlo, Albany County, New-York. They had been married but about two years, when a little daughter blessed their union. This little innocent was born but to bloom for a few short months upon earth, before her Heavenly Father called her to himself. It may be the earthly parents loved the child too fondly, with too exclusive a devotion, and God took away their idol. She had just begun to lisp the endearing words—Father! Mother!—Just budded in infantile beauty and sportiveness, when the stern mandate was issued; and disease attacked the delicate frame; the bright eye grew dim; the prattling tongue was stilled; the merry laugh was changed to that silence which the last trumpet only shall break.

She was two years, one month, and ten days old when she died. The only child—it was a bitter bereavement, and the parents sorrowed as those without hope. Not for a long period could they be resigned to this terrible affliction, and with humble faith say, Thy will, O Lord, not mine be done! Yet time brought its accustomed consolations, and they learned to think more that the loved one was present in heaven, and less that it was lost to earth.

I was the second child of my parents, and was born December 2, 1829. I was named Lucy Ann. As I was the only living child, it is not strange that I became their pet—almost a spoiled child. Well, years passed over my infant head, and at length memory began to show signs of an existence. And now for an incident, here and there, as that faithful friend may bring before me those happy days of youth. When care was a stranger, I was ofttimes strolling the little wood that was but a short distance from my home, and oft did I get lost chasing and searching for the little Robin red-breast as she warbled her lays at morn and eve; and, now and then, stopping to cull the wild flowers that thronged my pleasant pathway, till, tired and weary, I sank upon some mossy spot, and cried myself to sleep. But, by and by, I would be awakened by the call of my distressed mother; and away I would hurry to answer the summons, and gladden the heart of that fond one. But at length mother bethought herself of tying a bell on the little truant, and then her ear was gladdened by that tell-tale of my retreat. Time passes, and I hurry to my fourteenth year, and again find an observation. I was then at school, and possessed a temperament which made me foremost in mischief as well as in study. My delight in each was about equal. I was ever and anon trying to get my lesson, and, at the same time, thinking and acting mischief together. I would frequently contrive, during the hours of study, to read from another book, which I would conceal from the teacher's eye, and still have my lesson more perfect than half the scholars who were more studious, but less vivacious. It happened one night I was at a spelling-class that my train of thought was to take a different direction, for after school was dismissed, a Mr. William Smith asked to see me safe home. I at once took his offered arm, and away we tripped homeward, chatting and laughing at some foolish remark we might mistake for wit and sentiment. We at length were getting to be the objects of remark, as day after day passed in its turn; and we arranged business of almost every day so as to have an interview, which we would ofttimes while away in telling and laughing over the news of the day. But at length, father began to look after and into my love affairs, as he termed them; at the same time, he said I must discard Mr. Smith at once. To this, I answered nothing, but resolved to tell Mr. Smith father's commands, as soon as I should have an opportunity, which, by the by, soon came around. When I had told the story to him, he said father had no right to control or do as he had said. I, of course, was of the same opinion; and we soon found that we were in love, and vowed that nothing should or could be done to separate us. We, however, concluded to see each other no more for the present, for we had agreed to open a correspondence. As Mr. Smith's father lived in a tenant house of my father's, which was about a quarter of a mile from that in which we lived, it need surprise none that I received letters from Mr. Smith frequently, for Mr. Smith passed our door every morning, and our chosen post-office was under a large stone which was concealed beneath a large clump of May rose-bushes; so we corresponded in that way for a long time. But those things were destined to take a turn—the long concealed plans and letters were tale-bearers to a third and fourth persons. One day, I was going to make an afternoon's call, and as I was busy getting off, I accidentally left my key in the trunk which held those letters from the sight of any and all except the author and myself. After I had gone, my key was discovered by sisters Mary and Sarah, who were just wise enough to take a survey of my trunk and its contents. The result of course, was the discovery of a dozen or more love-letters; and all our sorrows and complaints became known. My sisters deeply sympathized with and pitied me, which roused my pride; and the result was, I got sick of the idea of loving Mr. Smith.

I will leave Mr. Smith for a while, and introduce a Mr. St. John to the reader. He was one of my old schoolmates. And one day, in the fall of the year, after school was closed, Mr. Smith and myself had accidentally met at a Mr. Stone's, at whose house I had called for the purpose of buying and carrying some very choice plums home to mother. As I knew that I should be reported to my parents if I should say a word or act in any way as if on friendly terms with Mr. Smith, I took it into my head to appear as cool as possible toward him that afternoon, hoping he would leave before I did, or not go home when I did, at all events; but I was disappointed, for as soon as I started for home, he walked along with me, and wished to carry my plums for me. I refused, and we walked on a little way and met Mr. St. John. He was riding for his health; and as he saw me carrying my plums, he offered to go back and carry them home. I told him it was but a little way, and I had already refused Mr. Smith's politeness, and turned to proceed on my homeward course, when he called to me, and said he had heard some news, and would, in a few days, call at my home and tell me the same. I bid him do so, and then walked on. Mr. Smith, in the meantime, had waited and heard all. I reached home in a few minutes, and then told mother all the news, and she finally said I was a good girl.

In a few days, I received a letter from Mr. Smith offering me his heart and hand in marriage, and requesting a positive and final answer. I accordingly penned a word in reply; told him I was not my own mistress yet, and as I was too young, I must be silent as to a part I felt I was not yet fitted to act. In a few days, Mr. St. John called, and said he had heard I was going to be married to Mr. Smith, and this is what he had heard and wished to tell me. I told him I thought there was a mistake somewhere, as I was ignorant as yet of any such thing. His keen eye was bent toward me as I made this reply; and I saw in that gaze a look that still seems to be written on the pages of the heart, and never can be forgotten. I can scarce analyse, now, the impression that look made upon me. Hope, fear, love, death—all seem to be blended in wild confusion as I recall that interview. I seemed to see a strange and gloomy future. I felt, when in the presence of Mr. St. John, an unusually gloomy and restless spirit, for upon that fair, young brow and cheek were written, as with a pen of fire, the marks of consumption! Days and months passed, and, by and by, came that messenger, Death, and tore from my young heart my loved, my beautiful one, and they laid him away beneath the cold ground! My heart had found its kindred spirit, but that spirit had soared away and found its mansion high. I could not yet follow; I must wait till I, too am called, and then may find that loved one, and be at rest forever!

About two years passed away, and I found I must apply my mind to exercises that would banish care and grief from its presence. I struggled with life's uneven way, and in a few years, I became acquainted with a George Washington Slater. He appeared an innocent sort of a boy; and as he was quite agreeable, I kept his company for some five or six months; and as I one night came home and found him there, I began talking and telling him that I should be obliged to discard him, as father was not willing that I should have any thing more to say to him whatever. As I turned away, I saw that all was not well with Mr. Slater, for, as pale as death, he stood partly leaning against the wall, watching me as I was talking with my cousin, A. Lobdell. I at length found myself alone with Mr. Slater, and I almost trembled to meet his pale countenance, for I felt such a pity for the poor fellow that I arose from my seat, and walked to where he was standing, and asked him what made him look so very pale. He made no reply, and I then took hold of his arm, and asked again what made him look so dejected and cold toward me. I met those sorrowful eyes bent upon mine with pity which I mistook for love; he pressed me to his beating heart, and a sigh escaped from his lips which marked and told that story that the tongue refused to utter. He again pressed me to his heaving bosom, and imprinted a wild kiss upon my brow, and told me a tale of how he loved; how he loved without one hope; how he had struggled to be free; and how vain was it for him to endeavor to forget me. I told him I would see him once more, and he tore himself away with a half hope; for it seemed to me as if a strange power, a wild and dizzy dream, bade me tell him I might and would allow him to visit me once more. He came again, and I saw a fever racking and torturing his frame. My father said he was love-sick, and tauntingly told me I had better have him, as he might die, or I might be disappointed, if, indeed, I was not despairing already. I left his presence, and walked into the other room where Mr. Slater was, and told him he had better try and get down to Mr. Hallock's, where he had spoken of going, for I well knew my father would rejoice if he died. He then arose, and went reeling away; and as I saw his retreating figure slowly lost to view, I wondered if he could bear the pain and anxious pity I then felt for him. Night came, and at nine o'clock, I retired to my bed-room, but not to sleep, for the God that made me gave me a tender heart, and nerved me with a daring spirit; I therefore waited till all was quiet, and then arose and dressed myself in my brother's clothes, stole out of my bedroom-window, and went to the stable, and took one of father's horses, and away I rode to learn what had become of Mr. Slater. I at length learned his whereabouts, without being discovered, for I saw some one was up in a room about 5 miles from my home. I at once alighted, and looked in at a window, and saw Mr. Slater and

some one standing beside his bed that appeared to be a
doctor. I then left and ran to where I had tied my horse,
and jumped upon his back with lighter heart than I had
when I dismounted, for I felt that some kind hand would
aid and take care of him. When I got within half a mile of
home, it commenced raining very hard, and I got as wet as
I could be. I was in a pickle as to what I should do to dry
brother's clothes; I therefore built a fire in the parlor, and
told mother when she asked me what I was doing, that I
felt sick, and was going to take a dose of hemlock tea to get
in a sweat; so when the tea was boiling, and I had got
warmed, and enjoying a perspiration, I felt quite well, and
brother's clothes were quite dry. I then retired, and soon
forgot all my anxieties and trouble. I awoke the next morning, and the sun's beautiful rays spoke in warm whispers,
not to be misinterpreted, of its Maker, God! When I appeared before my mirror, I learned how much an adventure
added health and beauty to the cheek. But in about a week,
I think, Mr. Slater came to father's again. And he looked so
pale and weak that I asked him to stop over night, for if, indeed, father meant and was determined to cross my way,
he should have a privilege. Mr. Slater informed me he had
been under the doctor's care since he left me last; how he
had broke his fever, and how very sick he had been. I went
out into the kitchen, and put over the tea-kettle to get him
some tea, for he said he had hardly eaten any thing since
he had been ill. I, after a long time, coaxed him to eat some
of my cookies, and at last I prevailed. We were in the sit-
ting-room alone, and brother came in and saw me combing
Mr. Slater's hair, and arranging it in its most-usual way; for,

reader, I pitied him because he had no home—no kind mother to comfort, or sister to care for him; they all were scattered over the cold-hearted world; his father was a drunkard, and long ago had left him; and thus poor George had no home. I, under these circumstances, resolved to be his friend, if I was driven from my father's house the next moment.

I will now attempt to give the reader a description of his person and report among the sons of men. He was rather tall, and of slender form; his hair of a jet black, and eyes of deep blue, and of an ordinary size; and as I looked upon him, I saw his eyes were clouded with sadness, and his pale, white forehead looked beautiful, but care-worn. I gazed in wonder upon one so beautiful, so innocent, and yet an outcast. He had heretofore had the name of being very industrious and cunning, which I knew was true to the letter. I felt I knew not how; but, in other words, that I was forming an acquaintance with Mr. Slater that I might repent if not carefully looked after. I therefore made up my mind to leave home, and go to a school then in Coxsackie, Green County, N.Y. I think it was in the month of June that I left off going to our District school, and prepared to go to Coxsackie, but before I left, I was expecting to see Mr. Slater again; I accordingly waited till after he came before I should settle the question. Well, at length the day came, and with it, true to his courage, came Mr. Slater. When father saw him coming in, I hurried him into the parlor, for fear he would say something to wound the feelings of George; but it seemed I was not destined to get off in this way, for in about an hour, father walked into the room with

a paper in his hand, and sat down and commenced reading. I saw a sneering glance was, now and then, sent toward
me and Mr. Slater. I arose in a few minutes and left the
room, and very soon after, Mr. Slater followed suit; and as
the moon, that bright sister of the night, was looking down
upon the earth in all her splendor, I put on my shawl and
bonnet, and asked Mr. Slater to take a walk with me just
out in the door-yard. He accompanied me, and I then told
him I was going to Coxsackie to school, and thought it
would be best to break off all our keeping company together, for I felt father was each day growing more bitter
against him. I told him to try and see if he could not love
some other more than me, for I knew that I was the first
lady that had kept his company. One thing I should have
stated in its proper place, that is, when Mr. Slater first came
to our house to pay me a visit, I asked father if I had better
receive his addresses; he said, yes; for, said he, if you treat
him well, he will feel himself somebody, and, perhaps, grow
to fill a respectable station; for, said he, he behaves well for
one so young. The consequence of my obedience the
reader has half read. Mr. Slater said he would abide by what
I thought was best. I then prepared to go to school at Coxsackie; and, in a few days, things had taken a change, and I
was at school.

Well, time passed slowly away, and I had not heard one
syllable from my George since I left home. I passed through
many little adventures while stopping there, and became
acquainted with but few, as I had but little relish for society,
except some particular friends that I there became acquainted with, by the introduction of my aunt, with whom

I was stopping. I received a letter one day from home, wishing me to come and make them a visit. I accordingly penned a reply, and told them when I could come. I at length went home, as I had appointed, and staid a week or two. I did not inquire for one whom I expected to hear from, nor did I hear a word about him. I could not bear to look around, for the old familiar scenes revived recollections of pleasant walks, merry tales, and innocent sports, in the company of one whom I could no longer see. The charm was gone while the charmer was absent. Memory of the old times made the present distasteful. I could not bear to stay there, and so I went back again sooner than I had expected when I started to go home. Father wrote and said if I wanted to live at Coxsackie he would sell out and come and buy there, if I wanted him to. I wrote him a letter and told him I was not going to stay there, and I at the same time told him of lands that were selling very cheap in Delaware and Sullivan Counties, and concluded by telling him a dream I had about the Delaware. I received a letter a short time after, stating father had offered his place for sale and was going a viewing in Delaware and Sullivan Counties with the intent of purchasing a place, if he found any to suit him. I was pleased to hear this, and wrote to father I would go with him if he purchased. In a few days brother came after me and told me father had gone a viewing; and so I went home again, and in three weeks I was living in Delaware County, with father, mother, sisters and brother.

I had been there but about a month or so when Mr. Slater came there, and all our former acquaintance was renewed. I then knew it was my time to talk to father in regard to Mr. Slater. I told him my design for coming into the woods was to avoid him. I told father he first told me to stay with George, and then, when I had won his heart, bade me break it. I told him my heart had no joy in him, for my early love was no more, and his dear remains were mouldering back to their mother earth; and as George was a good workman, and an innocent boy, I had told him I would have him if I could get your consent. This news seemed to sink deep in his heart, and he said he was afraid Mr. Slater would not use me well if I should have him. And he said he wanted me to wait till the next fall, and then if I still wished to marry Mr. Slater he would consent. I told him I would wait and was in no hurry to get married, if Mr. Slater was willing. He then said he would hire him to work for him and then I would have a chance to learn more of his true character. I told George what father had said, and asked him if he would not wait. He said he had come to marry me, as I had promised, and did not wish to wait. And to cut the story short, we were married, and father and mother had given their consent. It was too late now to repent or retrace my steps, nor did I wish to; for a while things went on very well, it seemed to all appearance, and I too late learned Mr. Slater's disposition.

It at length happened that a Methodist meeting was going to be held about two miles from our house, and as I wished to attend that I might learn the quality of preaching in the woods, Mr. Slater went with me, and after the preacher had finished his sermon, he said he was willing to preach again if any one sinner wished or would rise to have the brethren pray for him. At the end of this remark

Mr. Slater rose, to intimate his desire to be remembered. I also rose on seeing his wish to become a Christian. They then appointed a meeting the next evening, and we went again the next night, and they had an anxious seat, so called, for the inquirers to occupy that evening. I believe four others came forward and expressed a desire to get religion; and it seemed as if a revival had commenced at once. Those meetings continued for some two or three weeks, and at the end of that time Mr. Slater, myself, and twenty or more others, experienced and professed religion.

As the ministers had visited our house very frequently I had become quite a curious person for them to talk with, as my sentiments varied from theirs with regard to their belief very much. But they finally prevailed on us to have our names set on their class book; and as it happened one day, the preachers were both at our house, and I was telling and expressing my ideas as nearly as I possibly could, when Mr. Slater said he felt very much indisposed, and withdrew, and walked up to the chamber bed-room and laid down. I soon followed him and inquired if he did not feel any better. He said he did not, but affirmed his belief that he was going to die. I asked him what in the world had made him think so? He could give no reasons, I saw, but seemed and appeared so very strange. He then wished me to promise, if he died, that I would not marry again. I would not make a promise of so unusual and selfish a bearing. I laughed at him a little, and told him to go to sleep, and I thought he would feel better. I told him he was a strange boy, and coaxed him to try and sleep. He at length said he would, and I went down stairs again. It happened that when he came down he was

quite well, but appeared very cold towards me, and be-
haved very differently from his usual manner. Well, it happened the next Sunday that we went up to meeting, and
after meeting we went over with Doctor Hale and his lady
(a cousin of mine.) As we went to go home, we promised
to visit them some appointed evening that I do not now
recollect, but we fulfilled our appointment, at least; and as
the subject of religion arose for our discourse, Dr. Hale remarked that I was going ahead of the preacher in speaking
in meeting; and he said he thought I did wrong in speaking
after nine o'clock in meetings. At this Mr. Slater began, and
said I was going to leave him, and going off with the Do-
minie to help him preach. I made no reply to this false as-
sertion, but took up the Bible, then on the stand before me,
and opened and read aloud the sixth verse of the eighteenth chapter of St. Matthew, for it was the first sentence
that met my eye as I opened the Bible, which read thus:
"But whoso shall offend one of these little ones which believe in me, it were better for him that a millstone were
hanged about his neck, and that he were drowned in the
depths of the sea." I read no farther, but commenced weep-
ing, for I felt that that woe might be dealt on the heads of
my cousin and companion, for a great deal that they had
said I have not given place here—it is not my nature to af-
flict the afflicted. But truth must come if indeed I say any
thing; and now we will look and see where Mr. Hale is, and
how he felt after talking to me as he did. It happened that
we staid (George and myself,) all night with them, and as I
got up in the morning I saw that Mr. Hale was worried
about something, and at last he came to me and asked me

to forgive him, "for," said he, "I have slept but little all night, fearing I had wounded your feelings." I told him I could forgive him if my Heavenly Father could. But whether God has forgiven him or not is not in my power to say. But in a short time the news came to me that Doctor Hale was crazy, and soon after he was sent to the asylum at Utica. He appears to be quite rational at different times, but he is there now at the asylum, a poor crazy being.

I will attempt to follow Mr. Slater's proceedings. After my school had closed, (for I was teaching a district school at that time,) Mr. Slater and myself moved from our folks about two miles, I think in the month of March, for he had hired to work for a Mr. Levally, and so we lived in a tenant house of his. As Mr. Levally had a saw-mill opposite our house, Mr. Slater told me that Mr. Edwin Allen, the sawyer, wanted to board with us, and as he said he should have to be gone all day while he worked for Mr. Levally, I would not be so lonesome if Mr. Allen was there at his meals three times a day. I told him it put me to a great deal of inconvenience to board but one hand, as I should be at as much confinement in getting regular meals as though I had a dozen boarders; but however, if he wished me to do so, I would board him. So, in April, I think, Mr. Allen came to board, as Mr. Slater said we had ought to accommodate him. As I had a violin, and played it quite often, Mr. Allen, after a little acquaintance, would occasionally ask me to play a tune for him. I would sometimes play, as I did not wish to show any disrespect to persons, for when night came round Mr. Slater would come home with some half a dozen hands from Mr. Levally's and then he would get the violin and wish me to play. I would play, of course, but after a while I put my violin into the stove, for I had no relish for the society it was bringing. This did not suit Mr. Slater at all, and he said he would get another. I told him I would not play any more for a gang of card-players and swearers. He ripped out an oath, and said I could do as I pleased. In the meantime Mr. Allen was there, and as George came from his work he would begin some of his vulgar talk, and because I did not notice him or his speaking, he would appear sulky, and say but little, perhaps, the whole evening. Mr. Allen was a professor of religion, and we would converse together on some topic of a different character from the low one Mr. Slater had announced.

Things were permitted to go on in this style but a little while before I understood Mr. Slater's proceedings quite well; for he came home one day and said he was going to the depot store to get some tobacco, and should probably be back in a few hours, unless he went to our folks' house, and then he should stay all night. Night came, but no Mr. Slater, so I went to bed at about ten o'clock, for Mr. Allen had set up and been down to Mr. Levally's to see if Mr. Slater had not got back as far as there, for it was in the time of a freshet, and the creek was very high, and he did not know but Mr. Slater might have found the bridge gone away, and in attempting to get round to the other road have been lost in the woods, as it was a dark foggy afternoon and night. I felt worried, and after I had gone to bed I kept awake and could not sleep. It was about two o'clock, I should suppose, when Mr. Slater came in, with a lantern in his hand, and he came directly to my bed and asked me where Mr. Allen was. I told him that Mr. Allen and a cousin of mine, Mr. Smith were up stairs in bed. I made no inquiries as to the reason of his first question, singular as it was, only asked if anything had happened, or if he wanted Mr. Allen. He said no; and I dropped the subject as if nothing unusual was contained in the question. He soon came to bed, and I pretended to be very sleepy, for I saw and felt by his actions something was brewing. He at length began and said I had got so I would not speak to him now-a-days, if Mr. Allen was present. He said he had to work like a d—d slave now-a-days, and that I had tired of him. I told him Mr. Allen must be dismissed in the morning, as I would board him no longer. He hardly knew what to say to this reply, and he said as Mr. Allen's time was almost out I should say nothing to him, as people would think it strange if he went away.

I said it was strange, and as I had wronged him so much by not talking with him, and entering upon a subject I knew nothing about, as I had not been in the habit of talking on so unlearned a subject, I should not practice that art before Mr. Allen, and I accordingly heard no more about it that night, and when I awoke in the morning Mr. Slater had gone to his work. I know not what he thought, but I concluded he thought I would say nothing to Mr. Allen of his talk; but he was disappointed if he did, for I had told Mr. Allen previous to that night that I believed Mr. Slater was jealous of his being there, as I had learned by a great many unguarded remarks Mr. Slater had made; and now the actions of the preceding night spoke louder than words. Mr. Allen accordingly left boarding at our house right away.

And now I will pass over a few months and give place to the last story while I lived with Mr. Slater.

In the month of September, 1852, I was over to my father's one Sunday, and a cousin of mine, a Miss Helen Levally from Delhi, Delaware County, N.Y., was at Mr. Roderick Levally's, where Mr. Slater worked, on a visit, and she came with me the night before to our folks', and while we were there a Mr. Chandaler came to our house with a Mr. Thomas Smith, a cousin of mine, and a half brother to the Mr. Wm. F. Smith, my first gallant, as the reader will recollect in the first part of my history. Mr. Chandaler it appeared, came to our folks' for the purpose of inviting them, brother and sisters, to a quilting at Mr. Taylor's, some three or four miles from our folks'. He also gave Miss Levally and myself an invitation, and told me to invite Mr. Slater to a bee on the same afternoon, at Mr. Taylor's, as the gentlemen had a bee as well as the ladies, and then in the evening they were going to have a dance. I told him if Mr. Slater would come I did not know but I would, as Miss Levally was a stranger in the place, and said she would not go without I did, and as the quilting was to be that week, Friday, I had time to arrange matters in the respect. Thursday at length came round, and in the morning I asked Mr. Slater if he was going to the bee the next day. He said he was, and said he was going to wait on a Miss Yandes, and that I would have to get some one to wait on me if I went, for he had told me a few days before that I must go with Miss Levally, as she wished, as she was a stranger in the place, and a cousin. So, about noon Miss Levally came up from Mr. R. Levally's, and said Mr. Slater was going the next day to the

afternoon party, and as she had some errand over to a Mr.
John Spirbeck's, she wanted me to go with her and stay all
night, as Mr. Slater had given his consent; and as it was but
a little way from father's I could go there in the afternoon,
and then ride with brother and sisters, as they were going
as far as Mr. Chandaler's with their team. I told Miss Levally I had no objections, and could go as well as not, as I
was alone and had nothing to see to but Mr. Slater. She accordingly went back to Mr. Levally's and fixed and came
along for me about five o'clock. I went with her to Mr. Spirbeck's and stopped over night, and in the morning I went
down to father's and waited till it was time to start for the
quilting. Brother got up his ponies after dinner and drove
up to Mr. Spirbeck's after Miss Levally. They came back
in a few minutes, and sisters and myself were waiting and
ready to go. Now we will take one look at the party. Some
forty or fifty ladies, both young and old, had about finished
the quilting operations when we arrived, and we therefore
got there just in time for tea. We had an elegant supper as
good as the county was able to scare up. As I did not see
Mr. Slater appear, I began to conclude something was
wrong and out of tune somewhere. But I was not long to
be kept in conjectures, for a Mr. Buell Smith, a half brother
to Mr. William F. Smith, who was working at Mr. R. Levally's, came to me and asked how I enjoyed myself. I told
him as well as I had anticipated. I then asked him if Mr.
Slater had come; he said no. I asked him if he was coming;
he replied in the negative, and said Mr. Slater told him he
had not at any time intended to go; and that he said he did
not intend to go when he told me he was going; "for," said

he, "Mr. Slater said he wanted to make a fool of you just for the fun of it." I then felt he had some design in getting me to come, so I felt a little annoyed for a few moments, and then dismissed the matter and joined in the dance.

Well, in the course of the evening a gentleman asked me if I would play them a tune on a violin. I told him I would try; so the violin was brought, and all appeared to be attention, and I played some two or three tunes for the party. I received their acknowledgements, and then excused myself from playing more that evening, and the party broke up at a dark hour, which was just before day; and as it was about a mile over to Mr. Chandaler's, he walked with me, and brother and Miss Levally was with us in going to Mr. Chandaler's, across lots about a quarter of a mile to the railroad. We at length reached Mr. Chandaler's, and by the time brother's ponies were ready, it began to be day light. Miss Levally and myself were to stop at Mr. Yandes' and wait till Mr. B. Smith came along with Mr. Levally's team, as he passed there drawing lumber, and then, when he came back, we rode up as far as Mr. Levally's. I then went home, as it was but a little way from Mr. Levally's. I had been home but a few minutes before Mr. Slater came in. He began to tell me he had heard I had a beau last night, and that I had played the violin for the company. I told him that as he did not come, I had a right to engage an escort; and as I had been his tool for a fool, he could hardly make it appear I had done any thing but what he had intended me to do. At this he began to curse and rave like a demon; he at length stopped a minute, as I had remained silent, and asked when I was going to have another spree. I answered,

I thought I should go to father's that afternoon, as it was a pleasant day, and a Saturday too. He replied, he did not care where I went, if I went to hell; and after he had got through he went back to work again, and I went down to Mr. Levally's, and told Cousin Almira and Helen how Mr. Slater had acted, in part, and she cried, and told me she would not live and bear so much of him. She, Helen, then told me what he had said at the dinner table. He said he had given five dollars to be married, and that he would give five or ten more to be unmarried, which was a mistake; for he told me before I was married that he had some considerable money coming to him out at Westerlo, and that he could not get it when he left, as it was not then due; so finding he had no money to pay the marriage fee, I had told him brother would arrange and attend to those matters. I told brother, as I handed him some cash, to settle the marriage fee when we were married, which he did; and that was the way Mr. Slater paid the five dollars to be married. And, again, that amount he spoke of at Westerlo, I never heard or saw any thing of it whatever afterward. But again to my story.

Miss Helen said I must stop with her till morning, and then she would go over to father's with me; and so I staid at Mr. Levally's till after tea, and then George came in, and I told him what I had heard. He made no reply to it, but said I had better come along home with him, and stop my noise. I told him I had promised to stay at Mr. Levally's that night with Helen, which I did, for I was afraid to go back with him. That night I dreamed Mr. Slater stuck a knife in my side, which caused a great deal of blood to run from the wound. I dreamed I saw the blood roll down, drop by drop, which I have since found interpreted to the letter.

I went with cousin the next day to Mr. Smith's, the father of Mr. William S. Smith. As he is a second husband to mother's sister, I told her what had happened, and she said Peter (for that was her husband's given name) told her, when he came last night, he knew I would get a blast from Slater, for he had been to work that afternoon with him threshing buckwheat. I asked no questions as to what had been said, for I well knew Peter was an enemy of mine since I had refused to marry his son, William. While I was there, brother came in, and wanted to know where we were going. I told him I had started to go to father's, so he went back with us, for he had started to go to my house. When I got home, I told our folks how Mr. Slater had conducted himself in part; that I was afraid to live with him any longer. Brother said I should not go back any more, but might live with him the next summer, as he was going to build a house on his land, and then I should keep house for him; but father said I had better try and live with Mr. Slater since I was married to him. I told him I would try and do as he said, if he would let me move my things over and live at his house; for I told him that the house where we lived would not be fit to live in the coming winter, as it was so open and cold. He said I could move over if Mr. Slater would agree to it. So, in a few days, I rode over home to see how things got along. I found my house in confusion and shame. It appeared that Mr. Slater had been there, as I afterward learned, and got some of the neighbors to see what a wasteful and mean housekeeper I was; and to make this a point of shame, he had, that Saturday night I stayed at Mr. Levally's, went and made a fire and cooked some rice which he burned on the kettle; and as the next day was Sunday, he cooked some more in another kettle or spider, and then eat from all the dishes he could find, and left them all dirty, and looking anything but decent for the neighbors to see and charge to me. He had also milked the cow, and got the milk arranged in a manner to suit his time of inspection. He had not had the cow but a few days, but it afterwards, as you shall hear, helped him to make out his stories to my friends in Westerlo.

Well, when I saw Mr. Slater at Mr. Levally's that day, I found that he was willing to move me over home; so he went back with me, and drove the cow to father's, and stayed all night, and the next day he took father's oxen, and moved one load of things home. He then said he should be coming over there Saturday, and he could move the rest by hand. It happened to be rainy after that for a few days, and George came over to our house, and brother went up to a Mr. John Gearse's to get the beef he ordered. When they cam back it was in the night, and as it was very dark, they had got lost in the woods, and it was after nine o'clock before they found their way home. After they got home, mother cooked some beef for their supper; and as it rained now and then the next day, Mr. Slater stayed there, and was tormenting and laughing to see me cry, and mother was watching to see what he would do and say till, at length, she could bear no more, and she told him to leave her house instantly, and not to darken her door again till he could make up his mind to treat me a little better than a brute. He obeyed, and took some of his clothes with him, and went to Mr. Levally's, and told a few stories of how he had been misused by the whole family, which was false as it was told fair. He came over again on Sunday, and Mr. Thomas Smith and Mr. John Chandaler with him. He asked me for his clothes, and I got them for him; and when he got out of the door, he spoke and said he would give me his cow. I said, "Why, George, are you going off?" He said he did not know but that he should. I then said, "well, if you go, be a good boy;" and that was the last I saw of him till next Spring. After I heard that Mr. Slater had gone, I wrote a letter to my uncle, Truman Ingalls, who was living in Westerlo, as I supposed he would be likely to go there as any where. I will here give the reader a copy of the same;

Hancock, Monday, Oct, 24th 18[52]

Respected Uncle:

You will no doubt hear the story of Mr. Slater if he comes to Westerlo, as he has left this place in rather queer circumstances. Last Saturday, I have been informed, he left Mr. Levally's for Westerlo, or California, or parts unknown, without saying a word to me about where he was going. I wish you to ascertain, if he come to Westerlo, why he left, and, if possible, ascertain his complaints, as his actions go to show that there must be some cause for his leaving. Mr. Woolcoot came here, and told father that he had bought a cow which Mr. Slater gave me a few days before he left, and that he had paid Mr. Slater for the same. He drove her away a little while ago. George has moved me over to father's, and so I did not know what was going on; and he has left me with out anything to live on, except one bushel and a half of potatoes; and now as the cow has gone, I hardly know what to do; and as I expect ere long to become a mother, it seems to me that the Lord will prepare a place of rest in heaven for me—a poor, forsaken child; and I almost feel the assurance that He will take me to a place of rest ere long; and were I deprived of this hope, I, of all creatures, should be most miserable!

Please answer this as soon as you can, and let me know whether you have heard any thing in regard to Mr. Slater's departure or complaints.

P.S.—Be sure to have his statements entire, that justice and truth may yet triumph, and the guilty learn that there is a God that protects the widow.

Yours, respectfully,

L. A. Slater.

In a short time, I received the following answer, which I copy also:

Westerlo, Oct. 30t, 1852

Mrs. Slater:

We received your letter day before yesterday, and as an answer to your inquiry, George W. Slater arrived in this vicinity last Sabbath, and staid at Gardener Udell's that night. Mrs. Udell was here on Thursday, and told us the reasons he had assigned for his leaving you. The first and most serious charge was, that you went to sprees, and had other men to wait upon you home. Another was, that you would not do any thing; that he had got a cow, and you would not milk it, or take care of any thing; and also another, that your whole family misused him the worst way. These are the most prominent reasons that he assigned. He said that he had done all that he could to live; that you had seventy dollars of his wages and a cow. Another reason of his leaving you I should have stated in its proper place—that your family had driven him off; and he also stated that he thought if you was entirely away from your folks, he might possibly live with you. Buel has written a letter to Mr. Martin, stating that your family has misused Mr. Slater very much, the truth of which is best known to yourselves; and if you have taken any unjustifiable course with Mr. Slater, you alone will have to suffer the consequences. But I think you may congratulate yourself very much in that you have lived so long with him. You have exceeded my most sanguine expectations; and you may well feel consoled that you are no worse off, for it is easier to take care of one than a half dozen children. Bought wit is the best when not bought too dear; and now I know of no better way than to make the best of it, and to profit in the future, from the past, lest a worse thing befall you.

Yours, with due respect,

T. Ingalls.

P.S.—Mr. Slater was at Smith Lamb's on Thursday.

He bought a jewsharp and some hair-oil; he had candies with him.

So it goes, and so on, and so on,

This, reader, was the answer I received from my uncle. It so happens that I have a book-account of all the money Mr. Slater let me have, which was just ten cents, and that I took to pay the postage of his sister's letter. He commenced work at Mr. Levally's on Tuesday, February 14th, 1852, and was to have fourteen dollars per month, and left the place the 23rd of October, 1852. He lost over a month's work while at Mr. Levally's, and I wonder where the seventy dollars of his wages came from, that he said I had. I will tell you what became of his money—it went in a like manner, or similar one, that the cow did, and some of my things that he was going to move over to father's by hand— some were sold, and some given to Peter Smith, Esq., by George W. Slater; and as I have a book-account of all the articles bought by Mr. Slater for me, it amounts to something less than five dollars, and turns out to be less than the marriage fees he paid for; and as father has a book-account of the provisions he let us have when Mr. Allen was boarding with us, I imagine Mr. Allen paid the wrong man for his board when he paid Mr. Slater, as he told me he had paid him for his board; and this, gentlemen and ladies, is a sketch, here and there, of the treatment I received at the hands of a jealous husband. And has any one been guilty of setting Mr. Slater up? If so, they will be cursed for it. We read in the Holy Book, "Cursed is he that parteth man and wife." Has Mr. Smith had a word of news to tell Mr. Slater? If so, when Mr. Slater left, why did Mr. William F. Smith come and see me right away, almost, and say he knew I could not live with Mr. Slater, and tell mother if I ever went to live with Mr. Slater again to horse-whip me; and why did he send a letter to me, which I shall copy here for the reader to judge;

Coxsackie, May 24th, 1853.

Mrs. Lucy A. Slater

I must style you so, if once thought otherwise. I often think of the pleasure that I have taken when I had the happiness of your sweet company. Although it has been a long time since you and I took comfort together, and those days have passed and gone, still my mind often wanders back to by-gone days. I have often thought of a union between you and I; but the Lord has so seen fit that we shall never enjoy each other's troubles. You must write as soon as you receive this. Direct to William F. Smith, Coxsackie.

From one that will ever stand your friend as long as there is a drop of warm blood running in his veins. My love, to you, from your most affectionate friend,

William F. Smith

And, now, where do we hear Mr. William Smith is? We hear that he is sick and in a distant land, and among strangers; and as he has no money, he writes for his father to send him some; and we hear again that his father wrote to his dying boy that he could not help him; and we hear that Mr. P. Smith has yet another son who joined the United States Dragoon Company, and went to California. That son has deserted, as he is not yet of age. We hear that

Mr. P. Smith has a cancer that is speaking in tones not to be misunderstood, "Prepare to meet thy God!" Does it appear that any one has been "accursed" for sin? If so, these words are being fulfilled—"Vengeance is mine, saith the Lord, and will repay." And, now, reader, how think you I struggle with so much sorrow and disappointment. I lean upon the promises of the Great Jehovah; I can say, "Thy will, not mine, O Lord, be done." I have a clear conscience, and feel that if this earthly tabernacle of mine should be dissolved, I have "a building of God, a house not made with hands, eternal in the heavens!"

## Part II.

I am now going to relate some hunting stories; how I first was induced to learn to shoot.

I was in my tenth or twelfth year when I had the charge of some hundred chickens, turkeys, and geese, that I used to raise and sell, and then I had half the money I made in that business and in tending the dairy; and so when I went to Coxsackie, I had money I had made in raising calves and poultry to pay for my schooling, and all the expenses I incurred in going to school. In consequence of my keeping poultry, I learned to shoot the hawk, the weasel, the mink, and even down to the rat; so after I had moved to father's, and Mr. Slater had gone away, I used often to go hunting to drive care and sorrow away; for when I was upon the mountain's brow, chasing the wild deer, it was exciting for me; and as times were hard, and provisions high, I was often asked by father, who had become decrepid, if I could not go and shoot him some venison, as he was obliged to stop hunting. I used to feel sorry to see my poor father so lame, and hear him ask me to shoot him some deer. I at length put on a hunting-suit I had prepared, and away I started in pursuit of some meat.

Our little store of meat was almost exhausted, and I had hunted some length of time with but little success, till one morning I heard mother say we were quite out of meat; and when I had got ready to go hunting, I felt rather discouraged. So I wandered up the mountain that morning, without expecting to see anything, as usual, but as I got upon the top, I heard a stick crack, and I stopped and looked this way and then that, but could see nothing; so I started to go in the direction I had heard the noise. As I started, I saw a deer running as fast as it could jump; so I ran, too, for some twenty rods or more, after it, and then stopped to see if I could see anything of the deer. I looked about a hundred rods, and I saw a fawn coming towards me; so I got behind a log, and took aim at it, but the rifle did not go off; so I looked and saw that there was no powder in the tube. I primed her, and by that time the deer had got nearer to me; so I crept up to a log that was between myself and the deer, and took aim, and the rifle went off, and so did the deer. I began to think that I should have to coax the deer to me the next time, and hold the rifle against him in order to kill him. But I was not permitted to laugh at my stupid and wild shot long before I saw the deer drop down. I loaded my rifle again, and walked up to him. I saw he was dead; and close beside him, I knelt down, and offered up a prayer of thankfulness to my Heavenly Father that he had not forgot my toil from day to day, but had provided as we had luck. This was the first deer that I had the fortune to kill, and thus I had not got into the spirit of hunting much.

I recollect one night I was going to watch my deer-lick, and as it was a beautiful night for watching, a bright moonlight, I went up the mountain just before dark, and as I had a place of concealment, I sat there waiting for the deer. I had been there but a little while before I heard the bushes crack somewhere to the left of where I sat; so I kept as still as possibly and waited for the deer to come nearer. I at length heard one stamp, and then blow; I knew at once that they had smelled my track when I came up the mountain, and so I kept as still as possible and waited a little while. I had heard it thunder some length of time, but did not think that I was going to get caught out upon the mountain at night, and get lost. As I sat there listening to the concert of the deer, it, on a sudden, began to grow dark; I turned to look at the moon, and saw it was just going under some dark clouds then over my head. I jumped up to see if a shower was at hand, and saw a sharp flash of lightning that showed too plainly that I was swamped. I therefore started in the direction of the house, and as it began to sprinkle, I hurried along as fast as possible. In my hurry, I mistook my course, and instead of going east went north. It was very dark; I kept one hand before my eyes to ward off the bushes, and my rifle served as a cane to measure my steps down the mountain. I at length thought I was using rather a dangerous staff, as the lock might catch in a bush and go off; so I fired the contents I had destined for a deer away into the forest. The report reached the ears of mother, and she told our folks I was lost, for I appeared to be north of the house almost. In the meantime, I was slowly feeling my way down, as I supposed, to the creek that passes our door; but I found myself mistaken, for I came into a chopping, and, now and then, I found myself entangled in a brush-heap. I finally concluded I had got out on a creek that came from a pine swamp a little north of our house—some two miles. So I followed the stream down, and I could see, now and then, by the flashes of lightning, that I was going to have a time of it; so I hurried as fast as the darkness would permit, and at length I conceived I was within call of the house, so I gave a wild scream, and then listened for an answer from the house. In a few minutes, I heard the voice of my dear sister Mary. She and my mother had been listening and calling me for a long time, as I afterwards learned, before I hallooed. And, now, as I am penning this, it seems as if the wind's low sigh bears that welcome voice again to my ear; but, no, it is not so, for I know that I am far from my loved ones at home, struggling with my might to earn and give them a better station than is now their weary lot. But again to my story.

I answered the call again and again, till at last I saw a light coming toward me, I then, in a few moments, saw the forms of my brother and sister approaching. I stood still a few moments, and allowed them to near me; they came through the bushes pretty fast, and, ever and anon, sister Mary would call to get the direction of my whereabouts. We soon met, and I discovered that I had come off minus shoes and stocking-feet, as I had left them in the bushes some where. I was obliged to stop hunting a few days on account of sore feet. But I soon prepared to go again; and as there were moonlight nights, I went up on a clearing of brother's, some two miles from home, and watched for deer. I had been there but a short time, when I heard something coming which I knew to be a deer, for in a few moments, he made his appearance in the open field; and as I allowed him to walk round and round the field for the purpose of learning their manner of acting, I saw he was very careful, for he would just take a bit of grass in his mouth, and while chewing it, look around every way. He at last got within two rods of the rock on which I lay concealed, and then as I raised my rifle, the fellow jumped so rapidly, that I did not fire, for I thought he would stop in a minute; but [illegible] of the hedge ere he paused. I felt prov[illegible] hundred times for allowing the deer to escape in so [illegible] a manner, but it was a lesson for me afterwards.

I will now take the reader to an excursion on a cold winter's morn. The sun had not yet risen to warm and illuminate the cold earth, but I could just see sufficiently to climb up the mountain quite well. I crawled along very slowly, and was just raising the last hedge, so as to look over its summit, when I discovered, about twelve rods from me, an animal that I at once supposed to be a panther. As I looked at the fellow, he stopped behind a large tree, and appeared to be looking in the direction that I stood. In a moment, he started around the tree to come toward me. As soon as I got a fair sight at his heart, I fired, and O horror! such a noise as I heard in an instant caused my hair to stand erect, I believe, for I felt a cold sensation crawl over me that seemed to freeze the blood in my veins. The moment I fired, the animal turned and jumped, and ran out of sight; I reloaded my rifle, and ran after him. I was bothered so much at intervals to find his tracks, that I thought I would go back after chasing him a few miles. I supposed, from the appearance of things, that the ball must have hit him some where near the back-bone, as some places I saw where he had fallen down, and rubbed his hair off against the rocks and trees. It was snowing so very fast, that I relinquished the chase for that day, and went home. The next day, I started again. After I had been out about two hours, it again commenced snowing; but I thought I would not go back this time without taking a pretty good search; so I looked among the rocks and hills till about noon, as I supposed, and then thought I must go back so as to reach home by night. I was walking along very fast, when the idea occurred to me that I was lost, for I had long since ceased to find my track, and now it appeared that I was on a strange ridge of mountains. So I began to look around to find some familiar spot, or marked tree, but it was of no use; not a single thing could I find or recognise. I therefore fired off my pistols as signals of distress. I loaded and fired every little while and listened to hear my folks fire in answer some where; but not a sound could be heard save the whistling of the wind, as it drove the flakes of snow against my chilled frame. I then commenced running round and round, supposing, in the meantime, I was taking to a different course, till I came round to the place from whence I had started. At length I sat down in the snow to rest, and was startled to hear a distant sound somewhat similar to the noise I had heard the panther make the day before. I jumped up, and looked at my pistols and rifle to see if they were in order, and then started in the direction of the noise; I thought I might as well meet the panther as stop and freeze, for I had not a match with me to build a fire, and if night came on, I knew that I should perish with the cold; so I determined or rather courted to meet the panther again.

When I arrived at the spot where I had calculated the noise came from, I discovered the tracks of a man, and so I followed them, and in a few minutes, came out right above the house on a hill. I at once walked into the house, and mother said that father had just gone out with his rifle, supposing I had killed all the deer in the woods, having heard me fire so frequently near the ridge back of the house, not even dreaming that I was lost; so I stepped out doors, and fired off my rifle and pistols to let him know that I had returned. I had never before been lost in the woods in daylight, and so I was the more confused.

As I have greatly enlarged on the first part of this work, I shall be obliged to pass over some hundred little hunting adventures, and give them a place in my next book. But those days have passed, and I have left those happy scenes; for after the work of Mr. Talmage, the pedler, came before the public, in 1854, my hunting grounds were infested with hunters, and thus I was obliged last winter to hunt but little. I will copy his work here, as I may make truth appear convincing as it regards my present occupation:

Bridgeport, Conn., Jun. 2, 1853

MR. POMEROY—SIR: I received a letter a few days ago from a friend of mine, from this State, traveling as a pedler in the wild portions of Delaware and Sullivan counties, N.Y., in which he related an account of an adventure he had, which, if you think work the trouble, you will please correct mistakes and improper language, and give it a place in your paper. The story is as follows; I give it in his own words:

"I must relate an adventure that I met with a few days since. As I was trudging along one afternoon, in the town of Freemont, one of the border towns of Sullivan county, I was overtaken by what I, at first, supposed was a young man, with a rifle on his shoulder.

Being well pleased with the idea of having company through the woods, I turned round and said, 'Good afternoon, sir.' 'Good afternoon,' replied my new acquaintance, but in a tone of voice that sounded rather peculiar. My suspicions were at once aroused, and to satisfy myself, I made some inquiries in regard to hunting, which were readily answered by the young lady whom I had thus encountered. She said that she had been out ever since daylight; had followed a buck nearly all day, and had got but one shot and wounded him; but as there was little snow, she could not get him, and was going to try him the next day, hoping that she could get another shot, and was quite certain that she could kill him. Although I can not give a very clear idea of her appearance, I will try to describe her dress. The only article of female apparel visible was a close-fitting hood upon her head, such as is often worn by deer hunters; next, an India-rubber overcoat. Her nether limbs were encased in a pair of snug-fitting corduroy pants, and a pair of Indian moccasins were upon her feet. She had a good looking rifle upon her shoulder, and a brace of double-barrelled pistols in the side-pockets of her coat, while a most formidable hunting-knife hung suspended by her side. Wishing to witness her skill with her hunting instruments, I commenced bantering her in regard to shooting. She smiled, and said that she was as good a shot as was in the woods, and to convince me, took out her hunting-knife and cut a ring, about four inches in diameter, on a tree, with a small spot in the centre; then stepping back thirty yards, and drawing up one of her pistols, put both balls inside the ring. She then, at eighteen rods from the tree, fired a ball from her rifle into the very centre. We shortly came to her father's house, and I gladly accepted on an invitation to stop there over night.

"The maiden-hunter instead of setting down to rest as most hunters do when they get home, remarked that she had got the chores to do. So, out she went, and fed, watered, and stabled a pair of young horses, a yoke of oxen, and three cows. She then went to the saw mill, and brought a slab on her shoulder, that I should not liked to have carried, and with an axe and saw, she soon worked it up into stove-wood. Her next business was to change her dress, and get tea, which she did in a manner which would have been creditable to a more scientific cook. After tea, she finished up the usual house-work, and then sat down and commenced plying her needle in the most lady-like manner. I ascertained that her mother was quite feeble, and her father confined to the house with the rheumatism. The whole family were intelligent, well-educated, and communicative. They had moved from Schoharie county into the woods about three years before; and the father was taken lame the first winter after their arrival, and has not been able to do any thing since, and Lucy Ann, as her mother called her, has taken charge of, ploughed, planted, and harvested the farm; learned to chop wood, drive the team, and do all the necessary work.

"Game being plenty, she had learned how to use her father's rifle, and spent some of her leisure time in hunting. She has not killed a deer yet, but expressed her determination to kill one, at least, before New-Year's. She boasted of having shot any quantity of squirrels, partridges, and other small game. After chatting some time, she brought a violin from a closet, and played fifteen or twenty tunes, and also sang a few songs, accompanying herself on the violin, in a style that showed she was far from being destitute of musical skill. After spending a pleasant evening, we retired. The next morning she was up at four o'-clock, and before sunrise, had the breakfast out of the way, and her work out of doors and in the house done; and when I left, a few minutes after sunrise, she had got on her hunting suit, and was loading her rifle for another chase after the deer."

After the above piece was published, in many different papers, some people were curious to see and hear me play the violin. I, of course, would not refuse so trifling a request. But when the story began to be noised around, that Mr. Slater had reported, I found that I was subjected to the insults of wicked persons when I was traveling or away from home. And as Mr. Slater's story was false about my going to sprees, and having other men wait on me at home, and as the only "spree" I went to was at a Mr. Taylor's, I hardly admit that Mr. Chandaler waited on me home, for I think I rather waited on him home, as he was pilot no farther than his house, where my brother's wagon was in waiting. And that was the only time the [illegible] gave Mr.

Slater such a [illegible] about me. He well knew that nothing [illegible] touch my feelings like a report of that nature,
so he hesitated not to sink me, if possible, in the eyes of the
public and my friends. But I had a clear conscience, and I
waited to proclaim the truth. After some lapse of time, and
after my child was born, Mr. Slater came back, and pro-
posed living together again, as he said that at the time he
went off, he was almost crazy and confused. I told him that
I could take care of one child, and that I feared he might
get crazy again. So I thought it proper for him to wait a
while till he had become rich, as he said before he went
away, he should always be a poor man while he had me to
take care of; and as I thought that I could get along without
his care, he had better try and see what he could do. So he
stayed at Mr. Levally's some months, and worked very
steady. But as I was not to be shaken in my resolution, he
finally went off to Westerlo again to live. After living there
some length of time, he got some one to write a letter for
him to me, which I will copy here:

Westerlo, Oct. 5th, 1854

MISS LUCY A. LOBDELL,
    (As you call yourself, but which is Slater truly, but
I address you as you call yourself to please you,) in
truth, I wish it were as it was once—peace and har-
mony. Then I took comfort in my home, and in your
presence; but now you, perhaps, will not agree with
me. Let that be as it may, I will say that I am well, and
hope these few lines will find you enjoying the same
blessing. If you could but know the lonely hours that

I spend in Westerlo, you would have some words of comfort to send me. Aunt Becky is in this place, and said that you was sick. Sorry was I to hear that; but I hope that you will gain your health soon. [illegible] but how long you had been ill, I did not [illegible] to write as soon as you get this, and let me know [illegible] and that dear little child are. I long to see it once more, and if I hear favorable news from you, I will be in your place soon. But if you talk as if you would like to see the best friend you have in the world, you must say something favorable to me; for I do not wish to come and go to any place unless I am wanted. You must give my best wishes to your parents, and brother and sisters, and all inquiring friends. Tell them I wish to see them all. Now I will close, and say, I bid you do as you see best for yourself. You are capable of doing your own business; and I hope that you will not forget your best friend.

G. W. Slater

Well reader, I somehow could not swallow down the words "best friend." I too well understood the meaning. I had once before listened to his winning words; and when he had once got me within his bounds, you see a sketch here and there of his treatment toward me—the slave of my choice. My "wit was bought too dear" to be caught with smooth words which I did not believe; for I too well knew the plans of the destroyer. I too well have learned the form of the serpent when he would charm the innocent little bird till, step by step, it hops into the jaws of the reptile, and is no more. Well, after I received Mr. Slater's letter, I wrote a reply, stating to him that he might come and see his child; but, at the conclusion, said that I did not believe he would see me again; for I had made up my mind to leave after reading his letter; and as I had several reasons for leaving home, of which I shall treat on, I at once will state them. First, my father was lame, and in consequence, I had worked in-doors and out; and as hard times were crowding upon us, I made up my mind to dress in men's attire to seek labor, as I was used to men's work. And as I might work harder at house-work, and get only a dollar per week, and I was capable of doing men's work, and getting men's wages, I resolved to try, after hearing that Mr. Slater was coming, to get work away among strangers.

I accordingly got up one morning, and it seemed as if I must go that day. I did not dare to tell our folks my calculations, for I knew that they would say I was crazy, and tie me up, perhaps. So I went up stairs, saying I was going to dress, and go a hunting as I was accustomed to. I hurried and put on a suit of clothes, and then my hunting-suit outside. When I came down stairs, mother came toward me, and was going to take hold of me to see what made me look so thickly dressed. I saw her move, and stepped out doors saying that I must hurry, as it was getting late. I drove the cow up before I left, and then hurried up the mountain. I could not even kiss my little Helen, nor tell her how her mother was going to seek employment to get a little spot to live, and earn something for her as she grew up. So, I stole away with a heavy heart, for I knew that I was going among strangers, who did not know my circumstances, or see my heart, so broken, and know its struggles. As I was walking down to the Hankin's Depot, I met one of our dearest neighbors. He called to me, and asked me where I was going. I made no reply, but walked on; and I had got but a few yards, when I heard him say, "There goes the female hunter." I kept on walking in the meantime a pretty good pace, and then I stepped a little one side in the bushes to change my hunting attire. I in a few minutes saw some one pass the road who appeared to be in search of me. After the lapse of a short time, I walked out of the woods in a different direction, and went to Miss Hankin's, and she kept me over night. I arose in the morning at four o'clock, and walked to the Callicoon Depot, and bought a ticket for Narrowsburgh.

I must now leave the reader for a short time, and then I intend to write another book, in which I shall give a full account of my adventures whilst I adopted male attire; and as I am about to leave the reader for a short time, allow me to state the reasons for my adoption of men's apparel. The first reason, then, is this: I have no home of my own; but it is true that I have a father's house, and could be permitted to stay there, and, at the same time, I should be obliged to toil from morning till night, and then I could demand but a dollar per week; and how much, I ask, would this do to support a child and myself. I tell you, ladies and gentlemen, woman has taken upon herself the curse that was laid on father Adam and mother Eve; for by the sweat of her brow does she eat her bread, and in sorrow does she bring forth children. Again, woman is the weaker vessel, and she toils from morning till night, and then the way her sorrows cease is this—her children are to be attended to; she must dress and undress them for bed; after their little voices are hushed, she must sit up and look after the preparations for breakfast, and, probably, nine, ten, eleven, or twelve o'clock comes round before she can go to rest. Again, she must be up at early dawn to get breakfast, and whilst the breakfast is cooking, she must wash and dress some half a dozen children. After finishing up the usual morning's house-work, such as washing dishes, making beds, and filing the kitchen-floor, then comes the dinner as usual. Then comes the husband—the puddings have been burned a trifle when mother was busy at something else; then come complaints in regard to the pudding. Well, mother was busy with Bridget or Patrick, settling some quarrel or blows, and now mother has made father a little out of taste with the dinner. And this is the way the world is jogging along.

And, now, I ask, if a man can do a woman's work any quicker or better than a woman herself; or could he collect his thoughts sufficiently to say his prayers with a clear idea? No; if he was confused and housed up with the children all day, he would not hesitate to take the burden off his children's shoulders, and allow woman's wages to be on an equality with those of man. Is there one, indeed, who can look upon that little daughter, and feel that she soon will grow up to toil for the unequal sum allotted to compensate her toil. I feel that I can not submit to see all the bondage with which woman is oppressed, and listen to the voice of fashion, and repose upon the bosom of death. I can not be reconciled to die, and feel my poor babe will be obliged to toil and feel the wrongs that are unjustly heaped upon her.

I am a mother; I love my offspring even better than words can tell. I can not bear to die and leave that little one to struggle in every way to live as I have to do.

Again, we see the girl that is obliged to work day by day, and has no home; we see that one toil on—on—on; and the scene becomes changed. We behold her married for the sake of getting a home. Well, suppose we look into that home for a short period—what do we perceive? For a short period, we discover that all is very well. At length, the man becomes tired of being a home, for some reason or another. Perhaps he does not find it quite so pleasing to sit at home in the evening and hear the baby cry. It is less tedious to walk over to the hotel and learn the news, while mother loves her darling, and will try to soothe his sufferings into slumber; for, indeed, he is crying with pain, and can not tell why he suffers. Thus we see the home that our child has found. Ah! She indeed has found a home—a habitation of care and sorrow! She indeed hugs the cords that bind her there. Again, the husband comes home a little the worse for wine or rum. The mother marks that staggering form as he wends his way to bed whereon he goes to sleep and forgets the care he now throws away in the whirl of drunkenness. Mother clings tighter to that babe, and cries to that Being of Wisdom to enable her to bear the ills that thus betide her. Well, we will follow yet a little farther, We behold that the father has squandered all his living in drunkenness. He has become a drunkard; his home is now a hovel of wretchedness and misery. The mother is obliged to toil, day by day, for her little ones, and she can scarcely get a morsel of food for herself, as she will toil and feed on the crumbs. And, now, we see again that mother has fallen. Her babes are left to the charity of the world. They have no kind parent to kiss away the tear that courses down their pale cheeks; no mother to pillow their heads upon her heaving bosom. And when thus deprived of a tender mother, we need not wonder that our jails are filled with criminals. The warmth of a mother's love has long ago been extinguished; and thus the heart has had a sad blight thrown upon its life to make its darkness more terrible.

And now, reader, you have read, in part, a history of your unfortunate writer; but may God grant that you may never experience the sorrow I now feel. I am among strangers penning this little book. I am not permitted to lay the pen aside and kiss the child of my bosom. No; I am far away, struggling with my pen to lift the veil that has so long shrouded the hearts of fathers and mothers as regards the future for their offspring.

And now you, perhaps, are rich and have plenty. Could you bear to suppose that the little child you so fondly love should, after your body is crumbling back to earth again, be obliged to toil with the common class, and drudge, day by day, for a scanty livelihood, when, if you had been a prudent man, you might have foreseen and provided for the evil. Help, one and all, to aid woman, the weaker vessel. If she is willing to toil, give her wages equal with that of man. And as she bears her own curse, (nay, indeed, she helps to bear a man's burden also, ) secure to her her rights, or permit her to wear pants, and breathe the pure air of heaven, and you stay and be convinced at home with the children how pleasant a task it is to act the part that woman must act. I suppose that you will laugh at the idea of such a manner convincing; but I suppose it will not do to convince the man of feelings, who can see and pity, and lend a helping hand to release the afflicted, the child of your bosom, the choice of your heart, young man.

And, now, as I have done speaking of these bodies, these tenements of clay, let me speak of the spirit that dwells therein; let me tell you of a promised rest to the faithful; to those that serve God and love to serve him. Had I been deprived of a hope in this life, I could not have borne the keen arrows that have been hurled, and wounding me continually. But my Heavenly Father has protected and supported me in all my trials; and if I but meet the approbation of my Heavenly Friend, I shall not fall by the hand of my enemies. And now I must close with a few remarks; and as I am about to say farewell, permit me to invite you to choose my friend to go with, and support you through the short journey of life; for as the scriptures saith, "Man that is born of a woman hath but a few days, and they are full of trouble." It is a true saying, that every heart feels its own sorrows. Let me point you to one who will be a friend that sticketh closer than a brother; and for wisdom, search the Scriptures, for in them you have eternal life; and although I may never behold your faces in the flesh, I feel that I shall meet you at the great Judgment Day. And then how happy I should feel, if I, in writing this little scrawl, had persuaded a brother or sister, in the flesh, to love God, and keep His commandments, that they may have a right to the tree of life, and enter in through the gates to that great city. And though some do call me strange sort of being, I thank God

in whom I believe, and in whom I trust, and who is my de-
fence, and I can praise Him, that He has given me a heart,
that He will mould and fashion after his holy will; and as
nothing is more calculated to make a heaven on earth than
the love of God, I can say, that my affliction has taught me
a thousand truths of His loving kindness; for whomsoever
the Lord loveth, He chasteneth, and scourgeth every son
and daughter of Adam. And though the hand that has written this may crumble and mingle with dust again, yet this
work may remain as our works will follow us. And as the
present day and age of the world appears to be black with
iniquity, I would say take the Word of God for your counsel
and guide. If you love God and keep His commandments,
you will get to heaven in spite of professed preachers, or
churches, or the devil and all his dominies; and though
your name may be cast out as evil, you can rejoice, knowing
that if you but endure to the end you will be saved! Amen!

Your humble servant,
L. A. Lobdell

# LUCY'S LIFE AFTER
# THE *NARRATIVE*

THE ONLY DOCUMENT WE HAVE in Lucy's own words about her life and travels is her *Narrative*. After it ends, we can only map her footsteps with information provided by local and regional newspapers, court and other official documents, and oral histories. Although we are missing information about her day-to-day life, with the material provided we can draw certain conclusions. It is important to note that many of the accounts cannot be independently verified, were written long after the fact, or rely on a single source, often the same source repeated or reworded.

We begin shortly after Lucy has left her sleeping daughter Helen in the care of her elderly parents in Rock Valley, New York, in the mid-1850s. She would be gone for two years before she saw her family again. During this time she found her way to the small village of Bethany in Wayne County, Pennsylvania, about thirty miles northeast of Scranton. Assuming the name Joseph Israel Lobdell, she began to present herself as a man for the first time. She found work at a music school, where she gave singing lessons. She was held in high regard and was called a professor by her students.[1]

It was rumored that "Joe" was engaged to a young women from Bethany during this time, and that this engagement would abruptly end once a visitor from Long Eddy recognized the young teacher and identified him as Lucy in disguise. Lucy was forced to leave town, under threat that she would be "tarred and feathered" if she returned.[2]

With few prospects in New York and Pennsylvania, Lucy headed west to the Minnesota Territory. Land in the new territory was quickly being staked out by homesteaders and timbering companies. After the initial surveys were completed, the first public domain lands were sold. Lands in the federal territory were sold through public auction, private cash purchase, warrant entries, homestead and timber entries, and grants to the state and railroad. Each forty-acre parcel was sold to the highest bidder with a minimum price of $1.25 per acre. Homesteaders could obtain up to 160 acres of land by living on and improving their claim for five years. Claim owners would often hire individuals to guard their claim and ward off any squatters.

Lucy arrived in St. Paul as "La-Roi" and befriended Edwin Gribble, a homesteader with a claim on the north

View of St. Paul, Minnesota, including the capitol building, circa 1857, photographed by Benjamin Franklin Upton. (*Minnesota Historical Society*)

shore of Lake Minnetonka. The two became friends and lived together on the lake over the summer. Edwin Gribble at no time suspected La-Roi was a woman. Instead he only knew La-Roi as a young man from back east looking for employment and a claim of his own. Lucy soon got a job as a claim guard.[3]

Growing tired of waiting for the claim owner to return, Lucy sold her right to the soil to Gribble for a $75 rifle, and then traveled west for some seventy miles before stopping at a wintering place near the future site of the town of Kandiyohi, Minnesota. She was soon employed to reside on and hold possession of the new town site by some Minneapolis proprietors. By 1857, Lucy appeared in Manannah, Meeker County, a small town about twenty-five miles east of Kandiyohi, where she worked odd jobs, lived in a local boardinghouse, and still assumed the name La-Roi and dressed in men's attire. Lucy would live there for about a year before being arrested on the criminal charge of impersonating a man.[4]

The circumstances surrounding Lucy's arrest are not known. It is believed that the local law enforcement consulted the Blue Code laws of Connecticut in order to make an arrest and "purge the community of the scandal." Abner Comstock Smith, a federal attorney at the local land office who became involved in the case, describes the incident in vague terms some twenty years later: "In the summer of 1858, by accident, 'Satan, with the aid of original sin,' discovered and exposed [Lobdell's] sex."[5]

There is no explanation as to how her true identity was discovered—"by accident" and "original sin" may provide a clue, as a euphemism for Lucy's body being unintentionally revealed. County attorney William Richards added: "That, whereas, on Lobdell, being a woman, falsely personates a man, to the great scandal of the community, and against the peace and dignity of the State of Minnesota."[6]

Richards asked the court to make an example of Lucy to discourage others from following suit. Lucy stood trial in Forest City, a farming colony of about fifty people located about eight miles southeast of Manannah. Reverend and justice of the peace John Robson presided over her case. Ulysses Samuel Wylie, a young lawyer from Virginia then residing in Forest City, appeared with A. C. Smith as Lucy's defense counsel, and entered a "not guilty" plea. Following her trial, Robson cited the sixth-century Code of Justinian in ruling: "The plea of Not GUILTY was interposed, and the legal evidence to prove the necessary fact could not easily be obtained, and was left in doubt, and the court, after taking the case under advisement, finally ruled that the right of females to 'wear the pants' had been recognized from the time of Justinian, and that the doctrine was too well settled to be upset in the case at bar, and Mrs. Slater was therefore discharged."[7]

Despite her acquittal, the arrest and public exposure discredited Lucy in the small settlement and subjected her to vicious harassment. During her trial, Lucy had a mental breakdown. She remained in Manannah until she had recovered and was able to travel. In the *History of Meeker County* it is said that: "On recovering from the mental shock, she expressed a willingness to return to her family and friends, but had no means save her rifle, and nobody in the settlement able to purchase that."[8]

Meeker County would pay the expenses necessary for her return to her family in Rock Valley in the custody of a Captain A. D. Pierce. After her return, Lucy discovered that her daughter Helen had been admitted to the poorhouse in Delhi, about forty miles northeast of Rock Valley. Her parents were now in such poor health that they could no longer care for Helen, who was about eight years old. Lucy, now dressed in female clothing, traveled to the poorhouse to retrieve her daughter. There she learned that her daughter had been placed in foster care with the Fortman family of Tyler Hill, Pennsylvania.[9] At this point, it appears that Lucy suffered another devastating mental breakdown and at times seemed completely deranged. Lucy was still under the direction of Captain Pierce, who was under the

The poorhouse in Delhi, Delaware County, New York, c. 1900. (*Harvard Art Museums/Fogg Museum*)

impression he would be signing over Lucy's custody to her parents. Lucy refused to stay with her parents and asked Pierce to give her custody over to the Delhi Poorhouse, where she was admitted as an inmate.[10] Lucy's choice of the poorhouse over her own parents' house is rather troubling and gives a possible insight into her mental state at this time.

Poorhouses (alms houses), established by the government to assist the destitute, existed in the United States from about 1700 until 1900. The Elizabethan poor laws of 1601, which addressed relief for the poor in England, served as the basis of the system that developed in the American colonies, and is still reflected in the systems of today.[11] The poor laws established three principles: local responsibility for the poor, the requirement that people provide support to their poor; and the idea that towns were liable only for their own residents. In effect, the poor laws separated the poor into two classes: the worthy (orphans, widows, handicapped, and the elderly) and the unworthy (drunkards, petty criminals, the homeless, and the "lazy"). The poor laws also established the means for dealing with each category of needy persons and appointed the local government as the responsible agent for providing that assistance. Officials were given the authority to raise taxes as needed and use the funds to build and manage poorhouses, to supply food in their own homes for the aged and the handicapped, and to purchase materials necessary to put the able-bodied to work. If vagrants or able-bodied persons refused to work, they could be jailed.

The first poorhouse in New England was established in Boston, Massachusetts, in 1660. In 1766, Benjamin Franklin expressed his displeasure with public aid and poorhouses in general. After visiting the establishment in Boston, he observed: "There is no country in the world in which the poor are more idle, dissolute, drunken and insolent. The day you passed that act [the poor law] you took away from before their eyes the greatest of all inducements to industry, frugality and sobriety by giving them a dependence of something else than a careful accumulation during youth and health support in age and sickness."[12]

Poorhouses essentially became a dumping ground into which individuals of every description landed. The town drunkards, mentally ill, elderly, illiterate, and destitute were all grouped together in often overcrowded and unsanitary conditions.

From 1820 to 1900, there was considerable growth in the number of poorhouses in America. By 1890, there were

23,937 poorhouses in the Mid-Atlantic states alone. Some of these houses were small, housing perhaps a dozen residents. Between 70 and 80 percent of admissions were individual men, women, or children, while the remaining admissions were single-parent families. Many of the residents were admitted more than once, and sometimes several times in a single year.[13]

Over half of poorhouse residents stayed for more than three months, and about 10 percent of those who entered lived in the house for more than a year. Admittance to the poorhouse resembled that of a correctional facility. Residents were disinfected, their clothes taken away, their hair shaved or cut short, and a uniform was given to them to wear. Men, women, and children were kept together in the main house. The mentally ill were kept chained or shackled to the floor of basements or sheds. Each facility differed dramatically from others depending on the location and time period.

Lucy would be admitted to the Delhi poorhouse several times from 1860 through 1870.[14] The Delhi poorhouse was a two-story wooden building, situated on 175 acres of farmland. Over time, communities would implement a workhouse model in an effort to rehabilitate the poor and replace frivolous welfare use with productivity. Residents of the poorhouse, with the exception of the disabled and children under 7 years of age, were expected to perform labor. Work consisted of breaking rocks, grinding corn for flour, grinding animal bones for fertilizer, and picking oakem (used in rope making). These goods were then sold to cover the cost of their care.

The workhouse model had limited success. Disabled and mentally ill residents outnumbered the able-bodied, and poorhouses seldom covered their expenses. They deteriorated from lack of upkeep, and many were in debt. According to an 1857 New York State Senate report, the state's poorhouses "may be generally described as badly constructed, ill-arranged, ill-warmed and ill-ventilated. The rooms are crowded, the air is noxious and good health is an impossibility. Men and women mingled freely resulting in the offspring of illicit connections."[15]

With the majority of poorhouses being unsanitary, overcrowded, and unsafe for adolescents, politicians pushed for a new program to fund the poor. In 1862, Congress passed legislation for a Civil War pension program, which eventually made disability and old-age benefits available to all Civil War veterans and their families. This helped keep many veterans and their relatives out of the poorhouses. In 1864, Dr. Sylvester D. Willard led an inquiry into the conditions of the poorhouses and their treatment of the insane. He observed that:

> The investigation shows gross want of provision for the common necessities of physical health and comfort, in a large majority of the poor houses where pauper lunatics are kept. Cleanliness and ablution are not enforced, indeed, very few of the institutions have even the conveniences for bathing, and many of the buildings are supplied inadequately with water. In a few instances the insane are not washed at all, and their persons besmeared with their own excrements, are unapproachably filthy, disgusting and repulsive.

In some violent cases the clothing is torn and strewed about the apartments, and the lunatics continue to exist in wretched nakedness, having no clothing, and sleeping upon straw, wet and filthy with excrements, and unchanged for several days. The number of these cases may not be large, but there should be none such. There exists gross inattention to ventilation, and in frequent instances these unfortunates are denied even the fresh air of heaven. The buildings in many instances are but miserable tenements and were erected without any regard to ventilation. It is impossible from their very construction and arrangement to procure uniformity of pure air, and thus another great principle of health is denied. It will be observed that the returns not unfrequently mention the air of the rooms as "foul," "bad," "unhealthy."

In some of these buildings the insane are kept in cages, and cells, dark and prison like, as if they were convicts, instead of the lifeweary, deprived of reason. They are in numerous instances left to sleep on straw like animals, without other bedding, and there are scores who endure the piercing cold and frost of winter without either shoes or stockings being provided for them – they are pauper lunatics, and shut out from the charity of the world where they could at least beg shoes. Insane, in a narrow cell, perhaps without clothing, sleeping on straw or in a bunk, receiving air and light and warmth only through a diamond hole through a rough prison like door, bereft of sympathy and of social life, except it be with a fellow lunatic, without a cheering influence, or a bright hope of the future! Can any picture be more dismal, and yet it is not overdrawn.[16]

Dr. Willard's report would be instrumental in persuading the New York State Legislature to pass the Willard Act of 1865, which authorized construction of the first state asylums for the chronically insane. By the late 1890s, poorhouses in New York had all but been replaced with institutions and asylums.

Lucy, still residing at the Delhi poorhouse, soon befriended Marie Louise Perry. Marie was found at the train station in Hancock, New York, in the summer of 1865. She gave no destination to where she was traveling and had been put off the train because she had no money to pay further fare. Marie was the daughter of the highly respected Perry family of Lynn, Massachusetts. She told a station agent that she had eloped with James Wilson, an Erie Railroad worker, against her family's wishes. She then recounted a story of being deserted by Wilson for the daughter of the landlord where they were staying. The station agent kindly offered to start a collection for the unfortunate woman, so she could return to her parents. But Marie declined, and said she was too ashamed to see them, and ended up at the Delhi poorhouse.[17]

Census data from 1865 reveals that Lucy and Marie lived for a time at James Lobdell's house in Rock Valley.[18] However, Lucy and Marie would soon find themselves living a nomadic life in the woods of Pennsylvania on the other side of the Delaware River. Newspapers paint a varied picture of Lucy's life between 1865 and 1880, describing her as everything from a preacher to a lunatic. These articles are largely based on questionable hearsay, with little by way of credible, firsthand accounts. In an 1871 article in the *Stroudsburg Jeffersonian*, it is reported that Lucy was found by a fisherman, living in a cave with Marie. "The man was bare-headed and his clothing was torn and dirty. Accompanying him was a woman about twenty-five years old, shabbily dressed, but giving evidence of more intelligence than the man, who called himself Rev. Joseph Lobdell, and said the woman was his wife. As they walked about, the man delivered noisy and meaningless 'sermons,' declaring that he was a prophet of the new dispensation, and that the bear had been sent him by the lord to guard him in the wilderness."[19]

Shortly thereafter, an article entitled "Lucy Ann Lobdell" appeared in the *Wayne Citizen* which recounts Lucy's unsettling behavior.

> She was surrounded in the park by a large number of school children, and subjected to a process of chaffing which excited her to the performance of various antics. This procedure of the children being very naturally regarded by proper educational authority as demoralizing, and prejudicial to good order and discipline, it resulted in subsequently calling into requisition the penal resources of the school room; and the moral tone of the offenders was restored by a healthy larruping. One of the performances of the "female hunter" was climbing the monument in the park. She mounted to the side of the bronze veteran, embraced and kissed him, and talked to him in a sym-

Honesdale, Main Street. Photograph Postcard. n.d. (*Wayne County [PA] Historical Society Archives*)

pathizing strain. The next day she visited a school near Honesdale, and there made such a disturbance that she was removed and placed in jail.[20]

Her bizarre and erratic behavior during this time became a matter of public curiosity. The following account is given in the *Wayne Independent*, and demonstrates an interest in sensational gossip about Lucy (even when lacking newsworthiness).

THE MAN WOMAN: Lucy Ann Lobdell in Town
All tattered and torn, Lucy Ann Lobdell, the person who has created newspaper sensation, wandered around the streets of Honesdale on Tuesday last. On Monday evening, Reverend E. O. Ward of Bethany, discovered this strange creature on his front stoop, dancing and singing in a lively, wild, and reckless

manner. He recognized her as the person that years ago taught singing lessons in Bethany, passing herself successfully before the public as one of the masculine gender. She remained in Bethany during Monday night, and was next seen by John Hacker, while on his way driving from Bethany to Honesdale on Tuesday morning. As he drove to where she was standing, she immediately jumped into the wagon without an invitation, and instead of getting out again, commenced hugging bashful John in a free and easy style. Mr. Hacker drove to the prison in this town, and did not succeed in getting free from his female passenger in male attire, but by strategic reasons afterwards, she consented to part with him. During Tuesday afternoon she was to be seen on our public square in the vicinity of the soldier's monument; at one time she jumped inside the iron fence surrounding the monument and mounted the statue, embracing it in a loving manner, saying "I died for you." Poor girl, probably she thought of the man who wronged her years ago, when her now wrinkled face was fair as sweet sixteen. Then she was beautiful, with more than ordinary intelligence, but now haggared and insane, wandering through the country like a beast. Her garb consisted of white pants, dark coat and a light hat, and she seemed to be wild as the deer of the forests. She was last seen on the road leading north from town, on Tuesday night. Poor creature, nothing but death will relieve her from the suffering which she has endured since long years ago, when Henry [*sic*] Slater deserted her, leaving her and a two month old child which fate had to decree like its mother to be unfortunate.[21]

These events are further echoed by W. B. Guinnip in his 1924 memoir:

My second sight of Lucy Ann Lobdell was when she was brought before my father for disturbing the peace and being a public nuisance generally. This time she was hatless and without coat or vest. It seems she had come over into Pennsylvania from Narrowsburg [New York]; near the bridge she took the road that led to the settlement called Darbytown. A school house stood on a hillside along the way, among a grove of pine trees. Lucy Ann Lobdell decided to re-sume her girlhood occupation, for she entered the building and insisted upon "running the school." With a book she began cuffing the ears of the children and so terrified them that they hustled out of the door and ran down the hill at a lively pace, screaming as they went. S. N. Darby, owner of the tannery and store at Darbytown, then caused the arrest of the would-be-teacher. Lucy Ann Lobdell was committed to jail. There was no officer within miles to take her to Honesdale, so my cousin, Delos Guinnip, and I were delegated; he was to drive the team while I looked after the prisoner. On the back seat with me, Lucy Ann Lobdell sang and screeched. At times she tried to jump out of the wagon. She kept me on the move—about like a basket-ball player. John Ross was sheriff at the time, and he wasn't at all anxious to receive this prisoner. After reading the commitment he decided to take council. When Lucy Ann Lobdell saw him returning, once more she attempted to leap from the wagon, but I caught her by the shoulder and held on till I found out what he was going to do. "I will let her go if you aren't going to take care of her," I said. They had decided to lock her in Jail.[22]

Lucy would spend the night in the Honesdale jail, to be returned to New York the next day. Wayne County court registers during this time have no record of Lucy being convicted of any charge. Rather, it appears that she would simply be held briefly from time to time. Her behavior while in the Honesdale jail was still making newspaper headlines long after the fact. In a November 3, 1871, article entitled "The Lady in Pantaloons," Lucy was described as "singing songs of vulgar words, and climbing the iron bars across her cell window, even the prisoners that were in jail were made to blush at the sight, as she was perfectly naked, not a stitch of clothing could be kept on her person, her actions, and condition at that time not being fit to put in print, it would be disgusting to a New York Water st. slummer. She was continually singing or whistling organ-grinders' tunes. Captain Jenks seemed to be her favorite."[23]

"Captain Jinks" was a well-known song of the time:

> I'm Captain Jinks of the Horse Marines
> I feed my horse on corn and beans,
> And sport young ladies in their teens
> Tho' a Captain in the Army.

The old stone jail, Honesdale, Wayne County, Pennsylvania, left, and a cell, right. (*Ohliger*)

I teach the ladies how to dance
How to dance, how to dance
I teach the ladies how to dance
For I'm the pet of the Army

[chorus:] I'm Captain Jinks of the Horse Marines
I feed my horse on corn and beans,
And often live beyond my means
Tho' a Captain in the Army.

I joined the Corps when twenty-one
Of course I thought it capital fun
When the enemy comes, of course I run
For I'm not cut out for the Army.
When I left home, mamma she cried
Mamma she cried, mamma she cried,

When I left home, mamma she cried,
"He's not cut out for the Army."

The first time I went out for drill
The bugler sounding made me ill
Of the battlefield I'd had my fill
For I'm not cut out for the Army,
The officers, they all did shout
They all did shout, they all did shout,
The officers, they all did shout,
"Why, kick him out of the Army!"[24]

For the next eight years, Lucy would be arrested for vagrancy and jailed numerous times—and the newspapers would continue to exploit her condition. Articles announced whenever she was in town or arrested, or simply retold the story of the "Female Hunter" yet again. The sheriff of Honesdale even invited the public to come view her in the jail cell. A. C. Smith wrote this account in 1877:

"There." Said Sheriff Spencer, as he pushed open the ponderous door of one of the cells of the county jail in this place, "There is a woman with a history." On a low chair in a cell in the jail at Honesdale, Pa., July 20, 1876, sat a most singular looking person. A round, wrinkled, sun burned face, small head crowned with thick, shaggy gray hair that fell down over and concealed the blackest and sharpest of eyes; a slender body clothed in scant and shabby female garb, and lower limbs encased in tattered trousers. This was the occupant of the cell—Lucy Ann Lobdell.[25]

This account demonstrates well what an unfortunate spectacle Lucy's life had become. Although there was no expressed suggestion about her sexual identity, the fascination with her as a folk figure continued to revolve around her "masculine" attributes—wearing trousers, ability to hunt—and her bizarre behavior.

At this time, anti-suffrage propaganda had become a ubiquitous response to the women's rights movement. There were accusations that suffrage would undermine the family, with claims that women would abandon their children, become promiscuous, and wear pants. Fear was stricken into men with threats that they would be forced to do housework. Lucy surely embodied all that was wrong with the feminist lifestyle and the newspapers used her to that advantage.

Lucy's husband, George Slater, had died during the Civil War, so at some point Lucy's brother John convinced her to apply for a widow's pension. In February 1878, upon receiving and saving the pension, Lucy bought a small piece of property from August Yatho for sixty dollars.[26] The property, only about four acres, was located on the road leading from Narrowsburg, New York, to Branningville, Pennsylvania, in Damascus Township. Lucy and Marie Wilson built a small shanty, and worked picking whortleberries for shipment to New York and wintergreen leaves for August Yatho to manufacture wintergreen oil.

Soon after her land purchase, Lucy had to leave Marie to stay with her brother John. Lucy's daughter Helen and Helen's two children were already staying with John. There is no indication of the circumstances, but it appears

Lucy may have had another breakdown. She was cared for by John and her daughter, but by 1879, John could no longer take care of Lucy and returned her to the Delhi poorhouse. By this time, poorhouses were required to follow the Willard Act, which stipulated that inmates considered mentally ill must be moved to an asylum for proper care. The Delaware County Court held a hearing to determine whether Lucy was insane. Lucy's brother and some townspeople testified. The Court's decision* is as follows:

Delaware County Court
In the matter of Lucy Ann Slater a Supposed Lunatic
June 16th 1880

Memorandum of testimony taken in the above matter [at] the house of John F. Lobdell in the town of Hancock in [said] county. The following named persons having been called and sworn, To wit, Sidney K. Lobdell, [Str…][Spurback], Oscar Haight, Harry [Phiefer], George H. Milk, Stephen Ryder, [Ed…] Stephens, William W. Main, John Inman, John [Buckkapp], David Milk, [Amassa] Clark.

John F. Lobdell having sworn says:

I reside in the town of Hancock Delaware County N.Y. I am forty seven years old. I am acquainted with Lucy Ann Slater and have known her 35 or 40 years. She is a sister of mine. She is about 51 years old. She resides here in the town of Hancock in a house here

---

*The transcription of the handwritten document at the Delaware County Clerks office has brackets to indicate a word or name the clerk could not decipher as well as guesses in some instances of what an illegible word may be.

on my premises. I provide for her and her daughter and her daughters two children who live with her. Have provided for her going on two years, I should call her insane. She has been insane for more than ten years. Her mother was insane before her.

She has a habit of dressing in mens clothes. At times she has had spells when she imagines there are snakes in the room and [ ] and at such times she tears her clothes and the bedding in the room. She becomes quarrelsome and unmanageable at times and threatens to burn the buildings and runs off in the woods alone. She has a woman who she sometimes claims is her wife – this woman is also insane, from what I see and know of her she is of unsound mind at all times but she is at some times worse than at others. She at times uses very bad language. She has but one child a daughter whose name is now Helen Crawson.

She has spells and I [ ] each are about and in two weeks when she has [ ] [ ] spells. I know she has not sufficient understanding or ability for the government of herself or the management of her property. Nor does she have lucid intervals when she is capable of governing herself or managing her property. She has been in her present condition of mind for more than twenty years.

She has a small piece of land of four or five acres situated near Narrowsburgh in Wayne County Pennsylvania. I don't think it is worth more than $10. Is a very rocky poor place. She has no other lands or tenements. She has no personal property of any kind nor has she any interest in any real estate or personal property except the small piece of land I have mentioned. I think her insanity was to some extent caused by excitement in religious matters. She has never lost any children who died having children.

She [ ] [ ] where she now lives about March 1879. [Subscribed] & Sworn to before me June 16th 1880 Arthur More [Commission...]
John F. Lobdell

Ed L. [Pettingill] sworn says:

I reside in Hancock NY. I am a practicing physician. I have seen Lucy Ann Slater today. Never was acquainted with her before. I have frequently heard of her as a crazy female hunter. I have examined her today. I consider her insane to the best of my judgment. I should consider her incapable of governing herself or managing her property. I think her [ ] for any kind of [ ].
Ed L. [Pettingill] M.D. Subscribed & sworn to before me June 16th 1880, to me Arthur More [Commission...]

William W. Main sworn says:

I reside in the town of Hancock Del Co. I am about fifty years old. I am acquainted with Lucy Ann Slater and have known her for about twenty years. On one subject her mind is not sound but on other matters have heard her talk quite sensibly. I have never had an intimate acquaintance with her habits and customs. I know that she sometimes dresses in mens clothes and it is on that subject that I think her of unsound mind. I have lived in this vicinity about [ ] years and during that time she has been away most [ ] except about one or two years.

WW Main Subscribed & sworn before me on June 16 1880 Arthur More [ ]

[Ed...] Stephens sworn says

I reside in the town of Hancock Delaware County. I am acquainted with Lucy Ann Slater and have seen her more or less for the past nine years. I consider her from what I have seen of her insane. I do not think she is capable of governing herself or of taking care of herself. I don't know whether she has any property or not.

It has been the general talk ever since I knew her that she was a crazy person

[Edwin] Stevens Subscribed & sworn to before me June 16 1880

Harry Walsh sworn says:

I reside in Hancock N.Y. and have for about 22 years [last] past and have been more or less acquainted with Lucy Ann Slater for the past 20 or 25 years. Have met her a good many times and have seen her travelling along the road. The first that I discovered anything about Lucy which led me to believe she was insane was about 20 or 25 years ago when she was in her fathers saw mill sawing or attempting to saw. She was then dressed in mens clothes & particularly

attracted my attention [ ] [ ] was with me. We stopped
[ ] [ ] and from her appearance and [ ] at that time we
both came to the conclusion that she was crazy.

Some years ago I met her at [Mr] David [Kill...] in
Wayne Co Pennsylvania. I was satisfied then that she
was crazy. She was dressed in mens clothes and had
a gun and pretended to be hunting. After that I saw
her in company with another woman travelling along
the road. That woman was crazy. They both claimed
that they were man and wife and pretended to love
each other and that they could not bear to be separated. They then came to my brothers. He said they
frequently came there together in that way and
wanted to be together and sleep together. I saw her
once at Hancock with her husband at [ ] [ ]. She was
in the far room [ ] the men singing to her husband.
There can be no mistake but that she was then insane. I cannot swear positively that it was her husband with her. Have seen her at other times and think
she is insane without doubt and incapable of governing herself or of managing her property.
Harry [Henry] Walsh

Subscribed and sworn to before me June 16 1880
Arthur More [Commission...][27]

Despite the intended mental health reforms embodied
in the Willard Act, asylums were essentially prisons where
the mentally ill were abandoned by relatives or relegated
by the law. By the late nineteenth century, an increasingly
large number of women were being confined in public and
private asylums. Because of the lack of women's rights at

this time, women were often admitted for questionable reasons beyond their control. Mentally healthy women could be forced into asylums by their own fathers, brothers, and husbands for exhibiting "deviant" ideas and behaviors. These included progressive opinions on women's rights, gender roles, and unwillingness to marry and have children.[28]

Not only were women subjected to cultural and social pressures, they were also deemed likely to fall prey to disorders of the mind related to their biological vulnerability. Women were often diagnosed with "hysteria," from the ancient Greek concept of a wandering uterus (*hytera*, or womb), causing maladies involving physical symptoms better explained by psychological factors.

Once declared insane by the court, women would be sent away to the asylum with no legal recourse. The wide range of symptoms for which a woman could be institutionalized included gynecological disorders, religious excitement, overexertion, domestic troubles, childbirth, suppressed menstruation, epilepsy, senility, and tuberculosis. Treatments for these so-called symptoms of insanity included hysterectomies, blood-letting, induced vomiting, solitary confinement, lobotomies, leeches, hypnotism, and restraint in straitjackets.[29]

While Lucy was living with her brother, the outside world believed that Lucy had died. The *Wayne Independent* published this obituary on October 16, 1879:

Death of the "Hunter of Long Eddy"
News has just been received of the death of Lucy Ann
Lobdell Slater, known throughout the Delaware Val-

ley as the "Hunter of Long Eddy." She was the daughter of a Delaware river lumberman, and in 1851, at the age of 17 years, was married to George Slater, a raftsman. After the birth of her child, Slater deserted her and she donned male attire to seek her fortunes in the Delaware River counties in this State and of Delaware, Sullivan, and Ulster counties in New York. She built cabins at various points. Her supplies were obtained in exchange for game and skins. She wrote a book, detailing her adventures in the woods, and giving an account of her sufferings from cold, hunger and sickness. She recorded in this book that she had killed 168 deer, 77 bear, 1 panther, and numberless wildcats and foxes. Once she got up to singing school at Bethany in this State, and, while teaching the vocal art, won the love of a young lady scholar. Upon discovery of her sex the Bethany people threatened her with a coat of tar and feathers, and she fled. In 1868 she was joined by a woman named Marie Louise Wilson, and they hunted together until 1869. Then the former took the name of Joseph Israel Lobdell, and attempted to deliver backwoods sermons, in Monroe County, this State. They became nuisances and were lodged in Stroudsburg jail. In 1876 the two were living in a cave in the Moosic mountains, near Waymart, PA. While preaching in Waymart she was arrested and taken to the Wayne County jail. The Wilson woman wrote a petition to court for the release of her "husband" using a piece of split wood for a pen and pokeberry juice for ink.

The two were living together as man and wife at Mrs. Slater's death.[30]

Marie knew that the obituary was false. On August 5, 1880, the *Wayne County Herald* briefly recounted that: "The 'wife' of the 'female hunter' LUCY ANN LOBDELL was in town a day or so ago. She says that LUCY—or JOE—is not dead as reported, but is living in Delaware county, N.Y., with her daughter. The census enumerator at Hancock reports the Female Hunter as the only insane person in his district. She has now two grand daughters."[31]

Lucy was admitted to the Willard Asylum for the Chronic Insane in Ovid, New York, on October 12, 1880, where she would live for the next ten years.[32] Willard was a fairly new and progressive asylum for the time. The Willard Asylum was built in 1869 at the site of the abandoned Ovid Agricultural College. The facility had a 250-bed capacity, and would be filled just months after it opened its doors. Admission grew so quickly that it was soon necessary to renovate the old college building and eventually expand the entire campus. By 1877, Willard was the largest asylum in the United States with 1,500 patients.

Early patient treatment at Willard was referred to as "moral treatment." Patients were given nutritious food, clothing, exercise, and protection from the outside world. Patients who were able-bodied worked in the asylum's trade shops (sewing, basketry, and other crafts). The grounds included a farm with a dairy herd and vegetable garden. Nursing staff and night attendants were housed on the premises to guarantee that patients received the same care around the clock. Although the programs and amenities were a vast improvement over the poorhouses, the patients still were exposed to experimentation and treatments that would be considered abusive today, including electroshock, malaria-induced fevers, insulin-induced shock, and metrazol-induced convulsions.[33]

There were several medical directors who oversaw treatments at Willard over the years. Dr. Peter Wise would serve as the director for six years, beginning in 1883. During Dr. Wise's administration, he expanded the director's quarters and advertised the asylum as a tourist attraction.[34] Sightseers are said to have flocked to Willard to have picnics and be amused by the patients. At one point, there were so many sightseers that they overran the grounds and forced patients from the recreational areas. While it is unclear in what manner Wise personally benefited, what is clear is that the unprecedented manner of running the asylum was to the patients' detriment.

Dr. Wise would publish the following case study about Lucy in 1883.[35]

CASE OF SEXUAL PERVERSION.
By P. M. Wise, M.D., Willard, N.Y.,
Physician of The Willard Asylum for the Insane.
The case of sexual perversion herewith reported, has been under the writer's observation for the past two years and since the development of positive insanity. The early history of her abnormal sexual tendency is incomplete, but from a variety of sources, enough information has been gleaned to afford a brief history of a remarkable life and of a rare form of mental disease.

Willard Asylum, Ovid, New York. Main building and general entrance for visitors. Stereograph, 1875. (*New York Public Library*)

CASE.—Lucy Ann Slater, alias, Rev. Joseph Lobdell, was admitted to the Willard Asylum, October 12th, 1880; aged 56*, widow, without occupation and a declared vagrant. Her voice was coarse and her features were masculine. She was dressed in male attire throughout and declared herself to be a man, giving her name as Joseph Lobdell, a Methodist minister; said she was married and had a wife living. She appeared in good physical health; when admitted, she was in a state of turbulent excitement, but was not confused and gave responsive answers to

*She was actually 51 at the time.

questions. Her excitement was of an erotic nature and
her sexual inclination was perverted. In passing to
the ward, she embraced the female attendant in a
lewd manner and came near overpowering her before
she received assistance. Her conduct on the ward was
characterized by the same lascivious conduct, and
she made efforts at various times to have sexual intercourse with her associates. Several weeks after her admission she became quiet and depressed, but would
talk freely about herself and her condition. She gave
her correct name at this time and her own history,
which was sufficiently corroborated by other evidence to prove that her recollection of early life was
not distorted by her later psychosis.

It appeared she was the daughter of a lumberman
living in the mountainous region of Delaware Co.,
N.Y., that she inherited an insane history from her
mother's antecedents. She was peculiar in girlhood,
in that she preferred masculine sports and labor; had
an aversion to attentions from young men and sought
the society of her own sex. It was after the earnest so-
licitation of her parents and friends that she consented to marry, in her twentieth year, a man for
whom, she has repeatedly stated, she had no affection
and from whom she never derived a moment's pleasure, although she endeavored to be a dutiful wife.
Within two years she was deserted by her husband
and shortly after gave birth to a female child, now living. Thenceforward, she followed her inclination to
indulge in masculine vocations most freely; donned

male attire, spending much of the time in the woods with the rifle, and became so expert in its use that she was renowned throughout the county as the "Female Hunter of Long Eddy." She continued to follow the life of trapper and hunter and spent several years in Northern Minnesota among the Indians. Upon her return to her native county she published a book giving an account of her life and a narrative of her woods experience that is said to have been well written, although in quaint style. Unfortunately the reporter has been unable to procure a copy of this book as it is now very scarce. She states, however, that she did not refer to sexual causes to explain her conduct and mode of life at that time, although she considered herself a man in all that the name implies. During the few years following her return from the West, she met with many reverses, and in ill health she received shelter and care in the alms-house. There she became attached to a young woman of good education, who had been left by her husband in a destitute condition and was receiving charitable aid.

The attachment appeared to be mutual and, strange as it may seem, led to their leaving their temporary home to commence life in the woods in the relation of husband and wife. The unsexed woman assumed the name of Joseph Lobdell and the pair lived in this relation for the subsequent decade; "Joe," as she was familiarly known, followed her masculine vocation of hunting and trapping and thus supplying themselves with the necessaries of life.

An incident occurred in 1876 to interrupt the quiet monotony of this Lesbian love. "Joe" and her assumed wife made a visit to a neighboring village, ten miles distant, where "he" was recognized, was arrested as a vagrant and lodged in jail.

On the authority of a local correspondent, I learn that there is now among the records of the Wayne Co. (Pa.) Court, a document that was drawn up by the "wife" after she found "Joe" in jail. "It is a petition for the release of her 'husband, Joseph Israel Lobdell' from prison, because of 'his' failing health. The pen used by the writer was a stick whittled to a point and split; the ink was pokeberry juice. The chirography is faultless and the language used is a model of clear, correct English." The petition had the desired effect and "Joe" was released from jail. For the following three years they lived together quietly and without noticeable incident, when "Joe" had a maniacal attack that resulted in her committal to the asylum before-mentioned.

The statement of the patient in the interval of quiet that followed soon after her admission to the asylum, was quite clear and coherent and she evidently had a vivid recollection of her late "married life." From this statement it appears that she made frequent attempts at sexual intercourse with her companion and believed them successful; that she believed herself to possess virility and the coaptation of a male; that she had not experienced connubial content with her husband, but with her late companion nuptial satisfaction was complete. In nearly her own words; "I may be a woman in one sense, but I have peculiar organs that make me more a man than a woman." I have been unable to discover any abnormality of the genitals, except an enlarged clitoris covered by a large relaxed praeputium. She says she has the power to erect this organ in the same way a turtle protrudes its head— her own comparison. She disclaims onanistic practices. Cessation of menstrual function occurred early in womanhood, the date having passed from her recollection. During the two years she has been under observation in the Willard Asylum she has had repeated paroxysmal attacks of erotomania and exhilaration, without periodicity, followed by corresponding periods of mental and physical depression. Dementia has been progressive and she is fast losing her memory and capacity for coherent discourse.

Westphal reports that case of a female, that resembles in its salient features the foregoing; who, at the age of twenty, acquired regular desire towards her own sex. The sexual organs were normal and she practiced onanism. Having attempted to violate a female relative for the purpose of gratifying her desires and being repulsed, she became depressed with paroxysms of mania. He also reports the case of a male, and contributes an article with Dr. Servaes upon the same subject several years later. In a contribution and later, an exhaustive essay, Krafft-Ebing gives an analysis of the published observations of this anomalous and rare disorder to the present time.

With his own additions they number seventeen of both sexes and represent various degrees of perversion. In all but one of these cases there was a neurotic diathesis with positive symptoms of insanity. He discusses fully the relation of society to these sufferers and suggests they should be expected from legal enactments for the punishment of unnatural lewdness; thus allowing them to follow their inclinations, so far as they are harmless, to an extent not reaching public and flagrant offense.

It would be more charitable and just if society would protect them from the ridicule and aspersion they must always suffer, if their responsibility is legally admitted, by recognizing them as the victims of a distressing mono-delusional form of insanity. It is reasonable to consider true sexual perversion as always a pathological condition and a peculiar manifestation of insanity. The subject possesses little forensic interest, especially in this country, and the case herewith reported is offered as a clinical curiosity in psychiatric medicine.

Dr. Wise gleaned much of the information about his patient from newspaper accounts. Within his case study, we see for the first time the claim that Lucy thinks herself to be partly a man. The claim is made, although not directly quoted from Lucy, that "she states, however, that she did not refer to sexual causes to explain her conduct and mode of life at the time, although she considered herself a man in all that the name implies." She is however, directly quoted as claiming her genitalia as "more man than a woman." Dr. Wise reports after an examination that he sees no abnormality of her genitals but considers her to have a rare form of mental disease.

In the nineteenth and early twentieth centuries, homosexuality was widely seen as pathological disease, and homosexuality, along with cross-dressing and transsexualism, were more widely studied in Europe. Magnus Hirschfeld, a German physician, sexologist, writer, and researcher, wrote an influential case study on transvestites in 1910. However, he chose to conflate transvestitism with transsexualism, establishing an unfounded belief within his field that any person dressing as the opposite sex desires to change their sex.[36]

Dr. Wise published Lucy's case study in *Alienist and Neurologist: A Quarterly Journal of Scientific, Clinical, and Forensic Psychiatry and Neurology* in 1883. With this "rare" case study, Dr. Wise gained some notoriety within his field. The study ends with a final diagnosis by Dr. Wise that, "Dementia has been progressive and she is fast losing her memory and capacity of coherent discourse."

Over the ten years of her confinement at the Willard Asylum, the only records of Lucy are brief medical notes reproduced here in their entirety. The author is not recorded, but they were likely written by Dr. Wise.

The Doctors' Logbook
Lucy Ann Slater
Hancock—
Delaware Co.
Admitted, Oct. 12th 1880.

Age 56—Single Widow—N.Y.—Vagrant—Has had good common education. No religion—Said to be hereditary on maternal side—Insanity commenced over twenty years ago. The early history of her insanity is unknown. It is said she has worn male attire for twenty years. She claims to be a man at times. At other times she says she wears it because it is more convenient for hunting purposes—Has never been in an asylum, but has been in the county alms house at different times, and is now transferred from there.— She has usually been considered harmless & wandered about the country without molestation, but latterly she has made some threats of violence—...

When admitted she was in good bodily health, conversation was incoherent & actions silly. She was dressed throughout in male attire, and said she intended to continue to wear it. Dementia

The record states that Lucy Ann Slater was "brought from the county alms house" by its keeper, and the superintendent of the poor, on his order and by the medical certification of two doctors. A following entry, partially obscured, indicates that she "has been very much disturbed" at times, and that her physical health is poor, characterized by lung irritation and "severe hemorroids. Remains in bed." The logbook continues:

Feb. 23rd 1881. Hall # 2. Dorm. Condition has improved, and for the past two months she has been quite composed. Frequently wet and dirty at night. Occasionally destructive.

Jan. 7th 1882. Has had several periods of disturbance since the above. When she is excited she calls herself Jos. & when composed Lucy. Bodily health fair.

Aug. 3rd 1882. Is gradually becoming more demented, and erotic tendencies weakening. Her perversion of sexual inclination continues. She says she lived with Maria Perry for twelve years and wanted to marry her but Maria would not consent. She attempted to have sexual intercourse with her. At present she is incoherent & foolish—

Oct. 25th 1882. She has been disturbed for about a week. Her sexual perversion is not usually well marked; Bodily strength fair

Nov. 7th [18]83. Has been fairly quiet through the summer, and altogether more comfortable. Has had less sexual perversion. Dementia increasing. Practices masturbation and the practice is increasing. No menses.

Feb. 19—1885. When quiet talks quite well and is inactive. Excitement lasts for shorter periods and quiet lasts longer. Was slightly excited a short time since. When disturbed is wet and dirty at night, violent, talkative and noisy and inclined to cohabit with other patients, restless and sleepless, tears bedding. She is now quiet and good natured. Physical health good.

June 5—1885. Has passed through an excited period twice since last entry but neither of them were very marked. Transferred today to D. B. 4. Has slept in dormitory but on account of erotic tendencies needs a single room at times.

March 24th 1886. 2 D. B. 4—Since transfer has been usually quiet orderly, & pleasant, and bodily health good. Yesterday she had an attack of facial paralysis of the left side with loss of sensation & partial loss of motion in the affected side. Not much constitutional disturbance & refuses to go to bed.

April 6th 1887. Has apparently recovered from the above attack & is about the [illegible] as usual. Though at times complains of headaches.

Ap. 2nd 1888. Has been excited & restless & untidy a part of the year.

May 1st 1889. No change.

March 19—[18]90. Continues in good bodily health. Has improved somewhat & says "she has gotten over her old ideas." Has been quiet and orderly for some months past.[37]

Dr. Wise achieved the presidency of the New York State Commission on Lunacy, but his career at Willard ended with scandal rather than professional acclaim. New York governor Theodore Roosevelt removed him from his post for malfeasance—using his position to steal money from his colleagues, staff members, and other employees—in December 1900.[38]

Although Lucy did not die until 1912, premature obituaries continued to be published. One appeared in the *Honesdale Herald* in 1885, while she was still a patient at Willard:

July 2, 1885
Lucy Ann Lobdell – The Wayne County Female Hunter Dead.
Lucy Ann Slater, better known in this county as the female hunter, died in a New York State Insane Asylum on Saturday the 13th ult. She was born at Long Eddy, Delaware County, N.Y. in 1835 and early showed a predilection for out door life. It is said that at the age of ten she was a good shot with the rifle, and at twelve she chased a panther for miles through the woods killing it at last.

At eighteen her good looks, charming voice and skill upon the violin added to her other accomplishments, captured the heart of George Slater to whom she was married. He proved to be a worthless husband, deserting her and her infant child, a year afterward. The child grew to be the Mary Slater whose abduction, assault and attempted murder by George Kent and another, on an island in the Delaware river near Damascus, was described in these columns at the time of the occurrence.

The deserted and destitute wife left her baby with her parents and was next known in this neighborhood as a singing school teacher by the name of Joseph Lobdell, her fathers name. Many stories are remembered of the flirtations and trials of the gay young singest, but the secret of her sex leaking out, she abandoned society and took to the forests bordering the upper Delaware as a hunter. The woods in those days were full of game and it was not difficult to make a fair living by the sale of furs and venison, but with the clearing up of the country, poor Lucy found her occupation gone and latterly she has had a hard time of it.

Some twenty years ago, while in the county poor house, in Delaware county, N.Y., she made the acquaintance of one Maria Louise Perry, whose romantic history and misfortunes are also well known to the readers of the HERALD. A strange friendship sprang up between the two unfortunates. Mrs. Slater again took the dress of a man, and, as the Rev. Joseph Israel Lobdell, was married, so they claimed, to Miss Perry. For years they wandered about the counties of Wayne and Monroe in this State, and Delaware and Sullivan in New York—sometimes in the woods, often in the poor house and occasionally in jail as vagrants. Their constancy to each other in every trial and hardship enlisted much sympathy.

When "Joseph" was in charge of the authorities here as a lunatic, in 1876, his "wife" presented to the Court a petition so ably prepared as to secure the coveted possession of her "husband" and they went off in triumph together in Damascus township where they lived until poor Lucy Ann was sent to the asylum. The "wife" was peddling wintergreen berries in

Honesdale two or three years ago, but nothing has been seen of her here abouts since then.

Among the strange characters that have come into Wayne county history, the "Female Hunter" and her companion will always have a front seat.[39]

At some point, Marie became convinced that Lucy had indeed died. The following appeared in the *Honesdale Herald* in May 1886:

"The Problem of Life" . . . What the "apparent widow" of the Female Hunter has to say about it.

Some weeks since we made personal notice of the visit to town of the lady generally known as "The Female Hunter's Wife." The article appears to have met the eye of the person alluded to, and she has favored us with the following communication, which, though not intended for publication, so well expresses her views on matters of public interest, we take the liberty of putting it in print:

MR. HAM:—I met you in Honesdale May 18th, and having since seen some remarks in the HERALD of May 18th concerning me, am of the opinion that they were written by yourself.

Those remarks (of interest to me) need a little criticism, and are well worthy of comment. The kindly disposition manifested by the writer should not be treated indifferently by me; and the reason I have failed to evince to you that your efforts in our behalf have met my eye, is the inconvenient circumstances with which I have to do. I do not write this for insertion in your paper. I do not seek fame, but, as you kindly state, far prefer permission to work out unmolested my own "problem of life." Yet I am very sorry so long a time has had to elapse before I could use pen and ink for the purpose of expressing my appreciation of your kindly sympathy. I penciled these lines soon after reading yours, but only at this date find it convenient to forward them.

I am sorry you did not dwell longer upon "the avenues of employment" not being more "open" to persons of my sex.

If, instead of styling me "The Female Hunter's Wife," you had said "his apparent widow," I think the expression would have been more correct. I do not know why the companionship of two women should be termed "strange." The opposite sex are often seen in close companionship and friendly conversation, and, Mr. Ham, my sex are not inferior to yours.

"Not many may know the depth of true sisterly love."

Is not this a remark from your own sex?

If I have been "exceptionally educated," it must be because I paid my own tuition, board, clothes, etc., while at school apart from the common public schools. The public have misunderstood this fact, and for the sake of truth and justice it is time that the error was corrected.

I have never been seen in Pa. in my "proper dress." I have long known that it is unwise for woman to try to "protect" herself; for our Creator never designed

that she should, and our lawmakers have wisely provided for women in the event of her living singly after
she passes the age of 18 years. But, Mr. Ham, the
abuses and injustice which she often has to endure,
and which has such a crushing influence upon her
existence, seems to be wrong on the part of adminis-
trators of the law and the voters who create them. If
woman has no voice in the making of the laws of our
country, she should as a recompense, be granted sufficient other privileges to preserve her equality of
rights. How this is to be done, is the information
which many of the stern sex seem to need. Will you
find it convenient to inform them? You will thus
oblige, a friend and sister.

MARIE LOUISA. *The Apparent Widow.*[40]

Marie's life after Lucy is described by W. B. Guinnip,
who recalls: "Marie picked berries to sell and slept during
the summer wherever night overtook her. The people of
the locality were kind to her and she did not find it hard to
find some one to 'take her in' when winter came. Her bag-
gage for a long time she kept at the home of Reuben Comfort; and she has stayed for as long as a week at a time at
our house. But one day she said she was going back to
Boston, and started off intending to walk the whole distance. From that time to this nothing more has been heard
of her."[41]

After 1890, Lucy's care would be transferred to Binghamton State Hospital, the first institution designed

The Binghamton State Hospital, circa 1890. Lucy spent the last years of her life at this institution. (*Library of Congress*)

to treat alcoholism as a mental disorder when it opened in 1864, but it soon became a general asylum for any patient suffering from mental illness.[42] There she would remain for 19 years, 7 months, and 27 days before her death on May 28, 1912, at age 83. The cause of her death is listed as chronic endocarditis and manic depression psychosis. Besides a death certificate, there are no available records of Lucy's time at Binghamton Hospital.[43] She was buried in the hospital cemetery, with only a number marking her grave.

Lucy's proper legacy is just now coming to fruition. She has been the subject of much recent interest, due to

A cabinet photo of Lucy Lobdell produced by Kinch photographers of Walton, Delaware County, New York. The Kinch brothers operated a photography studio in Walton beginning in the 1890s. (*Wayne County [PA] Historical Society*)

the implications that she may have been lesbian, transgendered, or both. However, in interpreting Lucy's life, it is important to consider the historical record left behind. While there are some reliable accounts, we should proceed with caution in gleaning information from sporadic newspaper articles and the case study of a discredited physician who clearly had a flair for the sensational. In deciding who Lucy was, we should be careful not to allow presentism, emotion, or a sense of moral superiority to cloud our judgment. If we choose to view her life through a presentist lens, presuming that attitudes have advanced since that time, we are failing to understand what life was like so long ago, and give insufficient weight to the struggle of progress. Quite simply, some aspects of Lucy's personality and some years of her life remain a mystery.

So, was Lucy a lesbian? Was she transgendered? Did she simply have a misunderstood friendship with a fellow outcast, who happened to be a woman? Did she dress as a man out of necessity, convenience, and financial expediency? Was she mentally ill in her youth, or did social rejection ultimately drive her insane? These questions must be answered by the reader, after fairly considering and interpreting the record. Otherwise, we run the risk of further disrespecting and sensationalizing Lucy, and in the process doing a great disservice to this tragic but extraordinary individual.

# NOTES

PREFACE
1. "Death of a Modern Diana; The Female Hunter of Long Eddy: The Strange Life-History of Lucy Slater—Her Career as a Huntress, A Pauper, A Minister, and a Vagrant—Dressed in Man's Clothing She Wins a Girl's Love," *New York Times,* Oct. 7, 1879, Wayne County Historical Society Archives.
2. John William Ward, *Andrew Jackson: Symbol of an Age* (New York: Oxford University Press, 1955), 136–137.

LUCY'S EARLY YEARS
1. Michael R. Haines and Richard H. Steckel, *A Population History of North America* (New York: Cambridge University Press, 2000).
2. George Howell, *Bi-Centennial History of Albany: History of the County of Albany,* Vol. 2. Amasa J. Parker, editor, *Landmarks of Albany County New York* (Syracuse: D. Mason & Co., 1897).
3. United States Congress, Senate, *Annual Report of the Chamber of Commerce of the State of New York.* 1790–1910. Vol. 56, Vol. 61.
4. U.S. Government, Schedule I. Free Inhabitants in Albany County, Westerlo, New York. Census of 1850. Line 11.
5. James D. Folts, *History of the University of the State of New York and the State Education Department, 1784–1996* (Albany: New York State Education Department, 1996).
6. Folts, *History of the University of the State of New York and the State Education Department, 1784–1996.*

7. Leslie D. LaValley, *Basket Letters: A History of the Basket Brook* (Long Eddy, N.Y. : Basket Historical Society of the Upper Delaware Valley, 1990), chapter 63.

8. George Fox, *An Autobiography,* ed. with an intro. and notes by Rufus M. Jones (Grand Rapids, Mich.: Christian Classics Ethereal Library, 2000), chap. 13, "In the First Year of King Charles 1660."

9. *Illustrated Police News,* Sept. 20, 1890, 4. Newspaper.com Database.

10. Sally Soden, *Oral History of Irma Kimble Simons,* Dyberry Township, Wayne County, PA. 2005.090.1, p. 5. Wayne County Historical Society Archives.

11. *Bridgeport Standard,* Feb. 2, 1853. Newspaper.com Database.

12. "A Mountain Romance," *New York Times,* April 8, 1877, Wayne County Historical Society Archives.

13. "Death of the 'Hunter of Long Eddy,'" *Wayne Independent,* Oct. 16, 1879, Wayne County Historical Society Archives.

14. "The Story of the Female Hunter of Long Eddy," *Philadelphia Press,* Wayne County Historical Society Archives. *Bridgeport Standard,* Feb. 2, 1853.

15. "Death of a Modern Diana; The Female Hunter of Long Eddy: The Strange Life-History of Lucy Slater—Her Career as a Huntress, A Pauper, A Minister, and a Vagrant—Dressed in Man's Clothing She Wins a Girl's Love," *New York Times,* Oct. 7, 1879, Wayne County Historical Society Archives.

16. *Suidas s.v. Arktos e Brauroniois* (trans. Suda Online), Byzantine Greek lexicon, tenth century A.D.

17. C. G. Jung, *Collected Works of C. G. Jung,* vol. 9, part 1, 2nd edition (Princeton: Princeton University Press, 1968), 3–41.

18. Law Library of Congress, Married Women's Property Law, New York State Married Women's Property Law Act 1848.

19. Elizabeth Cady Stanton, *Eighty Years and More: Reminiscences 1815–1897* (1898; New York: Schocken Books, 1971), 52–55.

20. "The Lady in Pantaloons," *Wayne Herald,* Nov. 3, 1871, Wayne County Historical Society Archives.

## Lucy's Life After the Narrative

1. Janis Benincasa, *I Walked the Road Again: Great Stories from the Catskill Mountains* (Fleischmanns, N.Y.: Purple Mountain Press, 1994), 20.

2. Ibid., 21.

3. A. C. Smith, *A Random Historical Sketch of Meeker County, Minnesota* (Litchfield, Minn.: Belfoy and Joubert, 1877), 98–111.

4. Ibid., 105.

5. Ibid.

6. Ibid.

7. Smith, *A Random Historical Sketch of Meeker County, Minnesota*, 106.

8. Ibid.

9. Benincasa, *I Walked the Road Again*, 23.

10. Smith, *A Random Historical Sketch of Meeker County, Minnesota*.

11. Paul Slack, *The English Poor Law, 1531–1782* (Cambridge: Cambridge University Press, 1995).

12. Michael B. Katz, *In the Shadow of the Poorhouse: A Social History of Welfare in America* (New York: Basic Books, 1996), 23–27, 104.

13. David Wagner, *The Poorhouse: America's Forgotten Institution* (Lanham, Md.: Rowman & Littlefield, 2005), 67.

14. Smith, *A Random Historical Sketch of Meeker County, Minnesota*, 98–111.

15. United States Congress, Senate, *Annual Report Board of Commissioners of Public Charities*, vol. 36, 1860.

16. Sylvester D. Willard, *Report on Conditions of the Insane Poor in the County Poorhouses of New York*. Article XVII. Albany, N.Y., 1864.

17. Benincasa, *I Walked the Road Again*, 23.

18. U.S. Government, Schedule I. Free Inhabitants in Delaware County, Hancock, New York, Census of 1865.

19. "The Female Hunter," *Stroudsburg Jeffersonian*, Aug. 24, 1871, Wayne County Historical Society Archives.

20. "Lucy Ann Lobdell," *Wayne Citizen*, Nov. 9, 1871, Wayne County Historical Society Archives.

21. "The Man Woman: Lucy Ann Lobdell in Town," *Wayne Independent*, Oct. 1879, Wayne County Historical Society Archives.

22. Benincasa, *I Walked the Road Again*, 24–26.

23. "The Lady in Pantaloons," *Wayne Herald*, November 3, 1871, Wayne County Historical Society Archives.

24. Robert B. Waltz, *The Minnesota Heritage Song Book* (Minnesota Sesquicentennial Commission, in cooperation with the Fort Snelling State Park Association, 2008). www.MNHeritageSongbook.net.

25. Smith, *A Random Historical Sketch of Meeker County, Minnesota*, 98.

26. Wayne County Court Archives. Public Deeds. August Yatho et xo To Lucy A. Slater. 1878. 50/11.2. Wayne County Historical Society Archives.

27. Delaware County Court Testimony, Delhi, N.Y. In the Matter of Lucy Ann Slater a Supposed Lunatic. June 16, 1880. National Archives. Approved Pension file for Lucy A Slater, Widow of Private George Slater, Company G, 128th New York Regiment. WC259782.

28. Lynn Gamwell and Nancy Tomes, *Madness in America: Cultural and Medical Perceptions of Mental Illness before 1914* (Ithaca, N.Y.: Cornell University Press, 1995).

29. Robert Doran, *History of Willard Asylum for the Insane*, 9, 27–29.

30. "Death of the 'Hunter of Long Eddy,'" October 16, 1879, *Wayne Independent*, Wayne County Historical Society Archives.

31. *Wayne County Herald*, Aug. 5, 1880, Wayne County Historical Society Archives.

32. P. M. Wise, "Case for Sexual Perversion," *Alienist and Neurologist: A Quarterly Journal of Scientific, Clinical, and Forensic Psychiatry and Neurology*, 4, no. 1 (1883): 87–91.

33. Doran, *History of Willard Asylum for the Insane*.

34. Doran, *History of Willard Asylum for the Insane*, 30.

35. Wise, "Case of Sexual Perversion," 87–91.

36. Magnus Hirschfeld, *Transvestites: The Erotic Drive to Cross-Dress* (1910; Amherst, N.Y.: Prometheus Books, 1991), 3–27.

37. Doctors Logbook, Oct. 12, 1880–March 19, 1890, Willard Psychiatric Institute Archives, Ovid, New York.

38. State of New York, *Public Papers of Theodore Roosevelt, Governor 1900* (Albany, N.Y.: Brandow Printing Co., 1900), 195–199.

39. "Lucy Ann Lobdell—Wayne County Female Hunter Dead," *Wayne County Herald*, July 2, 1885, Wayne County Historical Society Archives.

40. "'The Problem of Life'—What the 'Apparent Widow' of the Female Hunter Has to Say about it," May 18, 1886, *Wayne County Herald*, Wayne County Historical Society Archives.

41. Benincasa, *I Walked the Road Again*, 25.

42. National Historic Landmark summary listing, National Park Service.

43. City of Binghamton, NY. Bureau of Vital Statistics Transcript of Death. Lucy Ann Slater. Record No. 301.

# BIBLIOGRAPHY

**PUBLISHED SOURCES**

Allderidge, Patricia. "Hospitals, Madness, and the Asylum: Cycles in the Care of the Insane." *British Journal of Psychiatry*. Vol. 134. 1979.

Bacon, Margaret. *The Quiet Rebels: The Story of Quakers in America*. Philadelphia: New Society Publishers, 1969.

Benincasa, Janis. *I Walked the Road Again; Great Stories from The Catskill Mountains*. Fleischmanns, NY: Purple Mountain Press, 1994.

Bolen, Jean Shinoda. *Artemis: The Indomitable Spirit in Every Women*. Newburyport, MA: Conari Press, 2014.

Brenner, Robert. *The Public Good*. New York: Knopf, 1986.

Capers, I. Bennett. "Cross-Dressing and The Criminal." *Yale Journal of Law and Humanities*. Vol. 20. 2008.

Comstock-Smith, Abner. *A Random Historical Sketch of Meeker County, Minnesota*. Litchfield, MN: Belfoy & Joubert, 1877.

Crowther, M.A. *The Workhouse System 1834-1929*. New York: Routledge, 2016

Diamant, Lincoln, ed. *Revolutionary Women in the War for American Independence*. Westport, CT: Praeger, 1998.

Doran, Robert E. *History of The Willard Asylum For The Insane and The Willard State Hospital.* Ovid, NY: Willard Psychiatric Center, 1978.

DuBois, Ellen Carol. *Feminism and Suffrage: The Emergence of an Independent Women's Movement in America, 1848-1869.* Ithaca, NY: Cornell University Press, 1924.

Fuller, Margaret. *Women In The Nineteenth Century.* New York: Dover Publications, 1999.

Gamwell, Lynn. *Madness in America: Cultural and Medical Perceptions of Mental Illness before 1914.* Ithaca, NY: Cornell University Press, 1995.

Guinnip, W. B. *Memoir. Oral History.* Pennsylvania. 1924.

Gurko, Miriam. *The Ladies of Seneca Falls: The Birth of the Women's Rights Movement.* New York: Macmillan, 1974

Hirschfeld, Magnus. *Transvestites: The Erotic Drive to Cross-Dress.* 1910. Reprint. New York: Prometheus Books, 1991.

Howell, George Rogers. *History of the County of Albany, N.Y., from 1609-1886.* Albany, NY: W. W. Munsell & Co, 1886.

Ingersoll, Charles A., ed. *Blue Laws of Connecticut. The Code of 1650; being A compilation of the earliest laws and orders of the General Court of Connecticut: The Constitution, or Civil Compact.* Cincinnati, OH: U. P. James, n.d. [ca. 1855].

Katz, Michael B. *In The Shadow of the Poorhouse: A Social History of Welfare in America.* New York: Basic Books, 1986.

LaValley, Leslie D. Basket Letters: A History of the Mountainous Region of the Upper Delaware. Reprint. Long Eddy, NY: Basket Historical Society, 1990

Lens, Sidney. *Poverty: Yesterday and Today.* New York: Crowell Co, 1973.

Lobdell, Julia Ardelia (Harrison). *Simon Lobdell—1646 of Milford, Conn. and His Descendants.* Chicago: Windermere Press, 1907.

Mayne, Xavier. *The Intersexes: A History of Similisexualism as a Problem in Social Life*. 1908. Reprint. New York: Arno, 1975.

Munsell, W. W. *The History of Delaware County, 1797-1880*. Albany, NY: W. W. Munsell & Co, 1880.

Slack, Paul. *The English Poor Law, 1531-1782*. Cambridge University Press, 1990.

Smith, A.C. *A Random Historical Sketch of Meeker County, Minnesota*. 1877. Reprint. Charleston, SC: BiblioBazaar, 2009.

Soden, Sally Eno. *Oral History of Irma Kimble Simons*. Honesdale, Pennsylvania. Transcription & Audio. Accession #2005.090. 2005.

Sutton, John. "The Politial Economy of Madness: The Expantion of the Asylum in Progressive America." *America Sociological Review*. No. 56. 1991.

Symonds, H. Ellis. *Sexual Inversion*. Basingstoke, UK: Palgrave Macmillian, 2007.

Wagner, David. *The Poorhouse: America's Forgotten Institution*. New York: Rowan & Littlefield, 2005.

Wise. P. M. "A Case of Sexual Perversion." *Alienist and Neurologist: Quarterly Journal of Scientific, Clinical and Forensic Psychiatry and Neurology*. Vol. 4, no.1. 1883.

GOVERNMENT DOCUMENTS AND ARCHIVES

City of Binghamton, New York
  Death Certificate of Lucy Ann Lobdell.

Delaware County Court, Delhi, New York
  In the matter of Lucy Ann [Lobdell] Slater a Suppose Lunatic. June 16th, 1880. Delaware County Clerks Office, Delhi, NY.
    John Lobdell Testimony.
    Ed. L. [   ] M.D. Testimony.

William Main Testimony.

Edwin Stephens Testimony.

Harry Walsh Testimony.

H. A. Gates, M.D., "Certificate of Insanity," signed Oct. 11, 1880.

Library of Congress

Married Women's Property Laws. New York State's Married Women's Property Law Act 1848.

National Archives

Approved Pension file for Lucy A Slater, Widow of Private George Slater, Company G, 128th New York Infantry Regiment (WC259782).

New York State

Board of Commissioners of Public Charities Annual Report. Vol 36. New York. 1860.

Chamber of Commerce of the State of New York, Annual Report. 1790-1910. Vol. 56, Vol. 61.

State Charities Aid Association Annual Report. 1874.

United States Federal Census

1850, Albany County, Westerlo, New York. Line 11.

1865, Delaware County, Hancock, New York. Line 8.

1860, Delaware County, Hancock, New York. Line 29.

1870, Delaware County, Hancock, New York. Line 16.

1870 Schedule I, Inhabitants in town of Romulus, In the County of Seneca. New York.

1880, Wayne County, Damascus Township, Pennsylvania. Line 10, 17.

1880, Delaware County, Hancock, New York. Line 15.

Wayne County Historical Society

*The Narrative of Lucy Ann Lobdell; The Female Hunter of Delaware and Sullivan Counties.* New York. Published for the Authoress, 1855.

Archival Photography Collection. No. 8592, 8593.
Wayne County Judges Book, December Term 1860-February 1876.
Wayne County Court Docket, 1847-1857.
Wayne County Court Docket, 1850-1855.
Wayne County Court Docket, 1860-1863.
Wayne County Court Docket, 1870.
Wayne County Continuance Docket, 1847-52, 1860-67.
Wendell, C. "The Willard Asylum and Provisions for the Insane." County Poorhouse Investigation. Legislative Printer. 1865.
Willard, Sylvester D. Article XVII. Report on Condition of the Insane Poor in the County Poorhouses of New York. Albany. 1864.

NEWSPAPERS & PERIODICALS

*Buffalo Evening News*
*Butte Weekly Miner*
*Cincinnati Daily Times*
*Cincinnati Enquirer*
*Harrisburg Telegraph*
*Herald & Torch Light*
*Illustrated Police News* (London)
*Kane Weekly Blade9*
*Kingston Daily Freeman*
*Leeds Mercury* (London)
*Little Falls*
*National Reformer Auburn*
*New Ulm Review*
*New York Times*
*North Star*
*Oneida Whig*
*Reading Times*

*Saint Paul Globe*
*Star Tribune*
*Stroudsburg Jeffersonian*
*The Lily*
*The National*
*Warren Ledger*
*Wayne Citizen*
*Wayne County Herald*
*Wayne Independent*
*Welsboro Agitator*

# INDEX